I0467919

75 Secrets Revealed on Productivity

Don't Work Like a Bull. Change Yourself in 7 Days

PART 1

Joe Martin

Disclaimer and Terms of Use: The Author and Publisher has strived to be as accurate and complete as possible in the creation of this book, notwithstanding the fact that he does not warrant or represent at any time that the contents within are accurate due to the rapidly changing nature of the Internet. While all attempts have been made to verify information provided in this publication, the Author and Publisher assumes no responsibility for errors, omissions, or contrary interpretation of the subject matter herein. Any perceived slights of specific persons, peoples, or organizations are unintentional. In practical advice books, like anything else in life, there are no guarantees of results. Readers are cautioned to rely on their own judgment about their individual circumstances and act accordingly. This book is not intended for use as a source of legal, medical, business, accounting or financial advice. All readers are advised to seek services of competent professionals in the legal, medical, business, accounting, and finance fields.

First Published, 2014

Dedication

To my 2 lovely daughters and my wife

Table of Contents

About the Author
Introduction

- ➤ 5 Secrets from America's Most Productive CEOs
- ➤ 5 Amazing Productivity-Boosting Apps
- ➤ 5 Habits that you Need to Change to Become More Productive
- ➤ 5 Design Secrets for a More Productive Office
- ➤ Get More Productive In Transit
- ➤ 5 Secrets To Be More Productive When Working from Home
- ➤ Say Goodbye To Email Overload
- ➤ Why You Must Join a Mastermind Group
- ➤ Let's Make Those Boring Meetings more Productive
- ➤ 5 Secrets to Work Like a Ninja and Save Time
- ➤ Brainstorm Ideas like Einstein
- ➤ Tackle the Humongous Workload like A Zen Master
- ➤ Spice Up Your Work Environment
- ➤ The Time Bandit Solution
- ➤ So Much paper, So less Time !

Conclusion

About the Author

Joe Martin is a life coach.

Earlier, he had set up a few businesses and sold them. He has a knack for writing and hence he became a full time writer. He has started his writing career with a hope to change lives.

When he is not working, he enjoys travelling, fishing, cooking and reading books. He loves to play with his two daughters when he is home.

He was featured on Google News, Yahoo Finance, Business Insider, The Boston Globe, CBC Money Watch and other popular media channels.

Introduction

DISCOVER:: How to Become More Vibrant at Work And Life

Do you want to become more productive but don't know how? Your willingness to buy this book alone proves that you are already motivated. All you need is some proper guidance to crack that **"CODE"**.

MOTIVATION + DETERMINATION + HACKS = PRODUCTIVITY

✔ You already have the motivation and determination to become more productive. What you need is some guidance along with a few tips. Here's where this book will help you. You are constantly trying to overcome procrastination, trying to fix your routine and yet there are a few loopholes you are trying to fix.

✔ It's true that not one book can be the ultimate guide to all your problems. Every author has something of his or her own to offer. I would highly recommend you to read as many books as you can from other authors.

First of all, thank you for buying my book.
I have broken down this book into 15 chapters. Each chapter has 5 tips.
Over the years, I have talked to many clients who were struggling to become more productive. I have written this book by keeping those problems in mind.
I hope you will find my solutions useful.

Chapter 1

5 Secrets from America's Most Productive CEOs

If your actions inspire others to dream more, learn more, do more and become more, you are a leader. -**John Quincy Adams**

To be inspired is great, to inspire is incredible.
The right words, said at the right time in the right way can work marvels in your life. They have the sharpness of a blade, which lets you carry out what you have always desired. Often, what happens is that we draw examples from our surrounding environment, which we assume to be inspiring. We try to emulate the success that we see around ourselves.

But what is important for us is to derive invigoration from people who have achieved great heights and strive for more. They set examples and teach us to never give up; we dream to live their lives.

Speaking of inspiring and motivating role models, I have here a list of tips from America's most innovative personalities. They have achieved insurmountable success, and yet, these are people who still say, "Be hungry for more."

Take to heart their words and advice:

1. Schedule your day:

Scheduling and making to-do lists give you an insight to how you should be spending the day. These organization tools help you cover many aspects of your work plan.

Danny Meyer, the CEO of Union Square Hospitality Group, says that he charts his work plan.

His next day is scheduled the day before it. Things to do, list of questions to be answered, appointments and other commitments for the next day are listed by his executive assistant before the end of the day. He then goes through them at night before his engagement the next day.

This way, he's not bothered by interruptions at work to remind him of small issues, and he doesn't have to worry that he's missing out on something.

Barbara Corcoran is a real estate mogul that turned $1000 into a multi-million dollar real estate firm believes in making a to-do list and ranking each task as A, B or C. This helps her prioritize her tasks for the day. Moreover, she is of the opinion that productiveness depends on preparation.

This incites pro-activeness and enhances productivity.

2. The Personal Touch:

This is about reaching out to people and interacting with them face to face. Such an amicable and attentive act makes people feel involved and drives them to deliver more.

Kevin P. Ryan, CEO of Doubleclick, believes in reaching out to his people. He carries a notebook with names of people in it and makes it a point to meet and talk to them every once a week. This helps in making his team coordinated into one and encouraging a feeling of oneness among his employees.

Communication is the key, and this is truly applied by Jordan Zimmerman of Zimmerman Advertising. He understands that through interaction via a phone conversation, he will prosper in his business.

3. Smaller teams:

Dividing employees into smaller teams helps in better management. Individual creativity is valuable, but often times, great ideas and products are born out of the thoughts of many people rather than just one.

In a quest to achieve decentralisation, Jeff Bezos, the CEO of Amazon, coined the Two-Pizza Rule, which expresses the need to make the size of teams no greater than the number of people it takes to eat two pizzas. To achieve productivity, it is good to break people up into smaller groups.

The urge to come to a decision before a meeting terminates made Caterina Fake of Flickr and Hunch fame to adopt a policy to make the agenda known before the commencement of the meeting. Fake requested that everyone drink half a litre of water before the start of the meeting; the goal is to finish the meeting before anyone has to visit the restroom.

4. Being Fit:

It is essential that you keep your body fit and healthy amid your busy schedule. According to Lord Buddha, "To keep the body in good health is a duty... otherwise we shall not be able to keep our mind strong and clear."

Jordan Zimmerman when once interviewed said that he hits the gym at 4 in the morning and finishes 25 miles on his bike before breakfast. Being in shape is what gives him energy.

Another workaholic, Mike Cassidy, CEO of Ruba, confirms the importance of workouts. According to him, they give him time to work alone on business and other problems, besides reducing stress and keeping healthy. He tries to conduct a non-work-related meeting while running or working out.

5. Quest for Hunger:

No matter how intelligent or laden with ideas and innovations you are, you should be driven from the inside. This quest for hunger to achieve what you aim drives you through thick and thin.

Steve Jobs said, "The only way to do great work is to love what you do." This leads to the question – if today were the last day of your life, what would you want to do? The urge to do the impossible and more makes you alive with newness.

The power of passion and the thirst to do what you love is what Mark Zuckerberg looks for in people. He once said, "Hire for passion, not skills alone, and treat your employees well."

Bill Gates once said, "If you're born poor, it's not your mistake; but if you die poor, it's your mistake."

There's always this insatiability that keeps all productive people gilded. Now it's time for you to develop this quest for hunger for your own germination.

Follow your passion, lead it with spirit, skills, and strive for continuous glory. I am sure you too can be that incredible success story that will inspire millions.

Chapter 2

5 Amazing Productivity-Boosting Apps

Be a yardstick of quality. Some people aren't used to an environment where excellence is expected.- **Steve Jobs**

With most people nowadays bustling through a workaholic lifestyle, they seek out various avenues to ease their burden.

Apps are designed to do exactly that. Today, there are apps for every purpose. In this era of automation and artificial intelligence, apps can do far better than what man could've imagined.

Using these apps can help you complete various tasks easily in a shorter span of time with less effort. So here are some beneficial apps that will help you boost your productivity.

1. Typinator

Typinator is an amazing app specially developed for the iMac. It saves the time and effort you spend typing; instead, you just have to key in the abbreviations and it lets the Mac fill up the rest for you. It replaces the words keyed in with the sentence intended to be typed, and it even works with graphics, dates, URLs and special characters.

It also auto-corrects typing errors and misspelled words. For all this to happen, you just have to define the abbreviations you are going to key in and what it has to fill up for you.

So you don't have to type in similar texts like salutations, contacts and directions repeatedly every day. The biggest advantage is the Auto-correction feature, which is helpful for correcting errors in American and British English, French and German.

2. Quickoffice

This app is developed for smartphones and tablets. Most smartphones allow you to open Word and Excel files, but things get difficult when you want to edit them. Generally, you would need a computer to edit these files, but this is where Quickoffice steps in. Quickoffice enables you to edit Word documents and XML spreadsheets on your phone, and creating or editing powerpoint slides in Quickoffice is a breeze.

It has the complete formatting tools. This saves you from having to load the documents onto a computer to make minor changes. It allows up to 6 documents to be open simultaneously, so text and images can be easily moved back and forth across these documents.

Quickoffice is integrated to Google Docs and Dropbox, so sharing these documents becomes even easier. But you cannot edit Word documents in the Drive, though you can view them. This is because Quickoffice and Google Drive are two different entities. So Quickoffice opens the documents in the drive as PDF files. Moreover it enables you to create Word, Excel or Powerpoint presentations on the go. The app has many additional features, but it is still easy to navigate through it. Setting up this app is also an easy task.

3. Mailbox

Many of us might be tired of looking through all your emails, waiting to be read. But what if we miss out on the important ones? Keeping this in mind, app developers have come up with an app called Mailbox. This helps you to manage your emails in an efficient manner.

When you want to archive the email, you have to swipe it to the right, and if you want to delete it, swipe it further to the right. Deleting emails is not a tedious job with Mailbox. If you see an important email but you want to read it later, swipe it to the left. This gives you the choice to save the email so that it will re-surface in the inbox after a particular period.

Also, this app lets you view all the earlier conversations in a chat-like view. Mailbox has integrated with Dropbox to come up with the Auto-swipe feature. This feature saves emails to be read later, directs particular emails to a list, or mutes conversations automatically.

4. Carrot

This is one of the most interesting apps I've ever come across. Developed for iOS, the Carrot To-Do makes the user schedule all his must-do tasks to help him complete them without procrastination.

Carrot is "the app with an attitude". It is a to-do list that interacts with the user and has a human personality. If the user keeps delaying a task, the app sends a message saying, "You do not want to make me upset".

When the user does his task on time, he gains new levels, which helps him unlock new songs, apps and bedtime stories. The navigation is also very simple; swipe down to add a new task, and swipe left after completing a task to remove it off the to-do list.

Carrot Alarm is also easy to use. To choose a time, swipe down, and to set the alarm, drag the ocular sensor. It wakes the user by playing funny messages like, "Wake up lazy human," and also plays one of the 30+ chart-topping songs already loaded in the app to sound the alarm. And to shut off the alarm, you have to do hilarious chores given by the app.

Carrot Fit also serves as your fitness trainer. It asks the user to enter his weight, calculates the BMI and allows the user to enter his goals. Periodically, it will ask the user to enter his weight. It will cheer the user when he loses weight and insult him when he gains weight.

5. Doodle

This is another amazing tool out there. Doodle allows you to send proposed meeting dates and times to all relevant members with a polling calendar. This allows each member to choose the dates and times he or she is most comfortable with.

Then, Doodle aggregates the responses and suggests which time is the best for the meeting. If Doodle cannot find a date and time that is suitable for all members, you have the option to suggest more dates and times. Plus, it allows the participants to communicate with the Comment feature.

Planning a meeting becomes a piece of cake with this app. Doodle works with Google and Outlook, so it will automatically synchronise the final meeting to your calendar.

With these apps, work will become lighter and more fun. There are more such apps to simplify various tasks, depending on each person's need.

So explore the world of apps and discover a whole new side to having fun with work. Good luck!

Chapter 3

5 Habits that you Need to Change to Become More Productive

It is better to lead from behind and to put others in front, especially when you celebrate victory when nice things occur. You take the front line when there is danger. Then people will appreciate your leadership. - **Nelson Mandela**

Who doesn't want a rewarding job and an ample amount of time as well? But the truth is, most of us with awesome jobs just end up juggling life and work.

Either we put everything into our job, or we get ourselves into a lot of other stuff in fear of stagnation. The end result is that we hardly have time left for ourselves.

We don't have a minute to think, appreciate life, and just relax. All this when continued for long periods can lead to grave mental and physical ailments. Increasing our productivity so that we always have extra time at hand for relaxation and recreation is the key here.

But how does one increase one's productivity without making major changes in lifestyle? One obviously can't give up some of the tasks, sit back and relax. So here are the things you need to avoid to manage your time better and increase your productivity manifold.

1. Procrastination

This is one of the main culprits behind lower productivity. We tend to delay our priorities for comfort or not-so-important tasks. We need to stop whiling time away and act.

Write down your priorities and attack them one by one. Be it tasks in the office or in personal life, start acting instead of thinking. Have you been thinking of hitting the gym for some months now? Get up and do it. You are anyway wasting time thinking over it.

So it's better to actually spend that time in the gym. One of my colleagues Martin used to just sit in the cafeteria and while away his time gossiping with friends. His attitude of "doing it later" resulted in him having to stay late every evening in the office to complete his work before the deadlines.

This obviously meant that he had no time for himself and his family.

Many of us have witnessed this. In fact, many of us belong to Martin's category. The simple idea here is to take charge of the situation and save the small talk for after the tasks are accomplished.

2. Not living in reality

Many of us live in a dream. For some, it is a pleasant one, and for others, it is a nightmare. The pleasant dreamers want to live in their dream only. They often think too highly of themselves and believe that they can get away with everything without doing anything.

The nightmare dreamers are of the view that everything is damaged and deranged, and they are therefore constantly dreading the next task, assignment, presentation or meeting. They often have low self-confidence. Both of these thought processes can be detrimental to your productivity.

Stop thinking too much and learn to live in reality and accept it; things will be much clearer then. Understand that you are not the best (or worst) employee around. With this attitude, your productivity will definitely scale up.

3. Saying "yes" all the time

Many of us are too scared to say "no". We tend to think that it will present a negative image of yourself, and people might feel that we shirk work.

But saying "yes" to everything will surely put you in a tight situation. This is because there is so much more to do than one can handle alone.

You will probably end up exhausted at the end of the day. This doesn't mean that you should stop owning up tasks and taking responsibility. It means that you should decide whether you can or want to do the task in question or not.

Look at your priorities and come to a conclusion. Often times, there are people who can do the job better than you.

So work only on those tasks that you can accomplish with conviction. And once you say "yes" to something, make sure you finish it to the best of your abilities.

4. Doing everything yourself

Some of us have this notion that no one else can do things better than ourselves. We don't trust others with work and would rather do it ourselves. But studies have shown that doing tasks in a group is more productive.

Not only do you get multiple hands and man-hours, but you also get different insights on how to approach the task.

The biggest job we have is to teach a newly hired employee how to fail intelligently. We have to train him to experiment over and over and to keep on trying and failing until he learns what will work. - **Charles Kettering**

It might be true that others may not know the work or task as well as you do, but try and delegate parts of it. You will not only save time this way, but also add to someone's learning. This in turn will help you the next time you face a similar situation. If you still can't think of letting someone else do your task, you can automate it too. A simple example is sending reminder emails.

There are various apps that will remind you of an unfinished task after a set period of time, until the task has been completed.

Similarly, there are various calendar-based apps that will help you prepare your schedule in no time. With the advent of technology, many complicated tasks can be automated as well.

5. Overworking

This one is a misnomer. You think that you are achieving more, but you actually don't end up with more results. In fact, the more you work overtime, the less your productivity will be.

Many studies have proved that working for more than eight to ten hours a day will actually be detrimental to your work. This is because the human body and mind have a capacity. While it is good to exert your body and brain, doing it for long periods exhausts them.

A normal human being needs time to sleep, eat and recharge the energy spent. If this is denied, you won't last long. In fact, it is suggested to break the monotony and do something else every two hours while working to re-energize.

By following these simple rules, one can boost one's productivity easily. Obviously, you need to stick to these mantras, as the changes can't be perceived overnight.

Now you can indulge in your hobbies, relax and even catch some extra hours of sleep with all the extra time you have at hand. So get up and get going!

Chapter 4

5 Design Secrets for a More Productive Office

Nothing will work unless you do. - **Maya Angelou**

Guys, why do we go to work in the first place? Money? Okay, point taken. But for how long?

After some time, when we've earned a considerable sum of money, then what?

During the first few years of a job, the salary is what drives us to go to the office. But after a certain period of time, that initial adrenaline rush gives way to monotony, and as a result, the productivity and work pace of the organization suffer.

This is a nationwide problem – everyone keeps complaining, but nobody wants to find the solution. Why not take some time out of your busy schedule and go through this article? Whether you are an employer or an employee, you can get ideas and generate your own.

1. Separate Cubicles

Employers need to understand that their employees are matured individuals, who need a little privacy and peace of mind while working. When we are talking about increasing productivity, we have to make sure that the employees are working in the best conditions in order to extract the best out of them.

So an open office does not tick the right boxes. There are too much people, chatting and loitering around. Even if one wants to concentrate on his work, he will face some distraction. Separate cubicles ensure a peaceful environment. Additionally, as-signed cubicles or groups of four or five in a cubicle allow employees to feel more 'at home' and secure while working. While there will be occasional breaks for a light chat, their concentration will fully be on the work.

They can also do up their cubicle in their own creative way. When conditions are good at work, the amount of effort each worker puts into his or her work increases, which in turn increases the productivity of the entire office.

2. Spacious Workspace

It is understandably difficult to assign a separate cubicle to each worker. What the employee can do in this case is to divide the workers into small groups based on their projects and work area, and assign a cubicle to each group.

But what the office managers have to keep in mind is that the size of a cubicle assigned to a group should be big enough. The last thing that an employee wants is a cramped space where he feels suffocated. We understand that employees do not spend all their working hours at their desk; it is not possible to work endlessly. They are humans after all.

They have to get up from their desk and take a stroll around the place. Imagine how a person would feel when he gets up from his desk to take a walk and has to give way to many others walking in the area or bump into another person.

So, it is important to give the office a spacious look and feel so that the little 'breaks' are smooth and work as a stress reliever, and also so that after the break when the person comes back to his desk, he will be able to give his best.

3. Proper color

The colors of walls affect our minds to a great extent. For example, when we are feeling sick, we tend to stay away from loud colors like orange or red, and instead prefer soothing colors. The office is the place where an individual spends most of his day, and he is getting paid for it. So the one who is paying would want the maximum value of the salary he is offering his workers.

For that, he has to make sure that the colors of the office walls are subtle and comforting. Colors that are too loud can get monotonous after a while. On the other hand, too much of soft colors make the worker feel lazy. Finding the perfect balance may be tricky, but it will be worth it.

4. Proper Lighting

Remember, an office is not a restaurant or a night club, so it has to be well lit. A dimly lit office or an office that provides too much of homely feeling can be the reason of a decrease in office productivity, because too much of a homely feeling can make workers lazy and too relaxed.

Bright lights in beautiful lampshades will keep the employees motivated to work and give their best. The productivity will increase exponentially.

5. Proper Canteen
Now this is the most important thing that has to be kept in mind. We all work to earn food; this is the basic truth. Food dominates most of our minds. After hours of working

hard, during the lunch break, all a person wants is a peaceful and fulfilling lunch.

The canteen is one of the most important area of an office; it should be designed properly and in a neat and clean manner, with tables, chairs, and table covers, all at the right places. The menu should be diverse. Okay, the workers do not need a five-star cuisine, but the food should be enjoyable and the price, a little less.

These five small tips can change the entire work environment while also immediately improving productivity and worker satisfaction. So, these five little things are all it takes to make the workplace a perfect place for working and fulfilling the primary purpose of working – that is, to increase the productivity.

Chapter 5

Get More Productive In Transit

The best preparation for good work to-morrow is to do good work today. **-Elbert Hubbard**

You're running, trying to catch that bus, but the problem is once you're on it; it takes you about an hour and a half to get you where you want to go. Or, you've gone to the airport early, and you're waiting for your flight; or you're on a journey across the country that requires you to sit in a train for two days.

All this time in transit is presumably wasted, but there are ways you can accomplish constructive and productive tasks while travelling. See below for 5 tips that will teach you how best to utilize transit time.

1. Catching up:

This is the time to return all those phone calls to relatives and friends that you have been putting off.

Make those calls now and get them over with; all you have is time, and since you won't be driving, it's safe to talk to them for as long as you or they want.

You never know how much wonderful news you might get, or catch up on all the gossip

2. Giving the brain some fodder:

Read books while waiting, whether it's an electronic book, audiobook or a paperback. Anything and everything you read will in some way or the other stimulate your brain and make you think about what you read.

In short, you'll never even realize when half the journey's over. Any and every kind of book, no matter the content, will keep you content while travelling.

Also, you may even write – perhaps chronicle some things that have been on your mind for a long time. Let it all out; it can be cathartic.
After all, J.K Rowling starting writing "Harry Potter" while travelling on a train. Now look at where that's gotten her.

3. For the busy bees:

For all those people who are constantly on their phones and email, thinking about work, the next meeting, and the closest deadline – take a deep breath and utilize this time to think about other things that can be done sans network.

Maybe you can write a report that is due, or finish some backlogged project; or, you can even organize emails, which you would normally never do with all those calls to make.

This could actually make your life easier if you take the time to organize your folders on your phone or laptop.
Make a list of things you need to do when you reach your destination that'll help you make the most out of the limited time you have there.

I have always argued that change becomes stressful and overwhelming only when you've lost any sense of the constancy of your life. You need firm ground to stand on. From there, you can deal with that change. **-Richard Nelson Bolles**

Or maybe even daydream about that much-needed vacation and draft an email in your head about how you'll be asking your boss for the holiday

4. Social skills:

Just engage in a conversation with the person sitting next to you. You will be amazed at what you can learn from other people, such as where they are going and how they utilize their time on long journeys.

You might make a new friend for just that hour, or perhaps even for life. However, you must be cautious and avoid divulging too many personal details about yourself; similarly, you must restrain yourself from asking the other person too many personal questions.

Be polite and talk about general things, unless the other person opens up and says something more.

5. Let it be:

So what if the travelling time takes up a part of your day or takes up two whole days? Let yourself go, relax, and take a nap.

Listen to some songs and just pretend you have nowhere to be for a little while.

Observe all the people around you; you'll see some interesting things. The different kinds of people who are in the bus with you for exactly the same distance somehow produces a feeling of solidarity, so enjoy that.

Catch up on things you cannot normally do because of work, or just simply relax. You need your energy, so let the rocking motions of the bus lull you into slumber, or just close your eyes and enjoy the wind and the slow music emanating from the ear phones.

Well, these are the five tips that are easy enough to indulge in while on the road. If you're in for the long haul, and stuck in the train compartment sleepless, take a look out the window and you'll be amazed at how beautiful the outside world looks while in motion.

It is not always necessary to actually be doing something to make every hour of every day productive; sometimes, not doing anything helps a lot more than completing all your daily chores. Meditating and just letting the breeze of the moving vehicle hit your face can comfort you in ways nothing else can.

Read a book, have a snack, listen to some good tunes, and engage with people. After all, being productive means doing what helps you.

So enjoy the alone time you get while travelling and engage in things that you absolutely must do and nothing more.

Chapter 6

5 Secrets To Be More Productive When Working from Home

It's like Forrest Gump said, 'Life is like a box of chocolates.' Your career is like a box of chocolates - you never know what you're going to get. But everything you get is going to teach you something along the way and make you the person you are today. That's the exciting part - it's an adventure in itself. **- Nick Carter**

Working from home is a recent trend. If you come to think of it as an option, you might wonder why not; after all, working from home gives you the independence that no job can ever give you.

Even though they might deny it, human beings don't like to be controlled all the time. While working from home gives one joy, it brings up the discomfort of procrastination and ignorance. Furthermore, it raises the question of how to enhance productivity while working from home without overburdening yourself. Here are a few tips that you might consider to make working from home more productive.

1. Know yourself

Before starting your work, you need to take into consideration the various questions that make you think deeply, such as: what kind of environment do you need for working? What is the best time to work?

What work do you do before, and how do you discipline yourself? What do you really want to do, and how do you overcome the fear of incompletion of targets?

Once you find the answers to all of these questions, it becomes easy to manage your work. Finding answers is essential, but equally important is applying them and solving them.

Once you're clear of all the things you really want, it becomes simple to proceed further. Identify what needs to get done every day and make sure you do it.

2. Plan your work

Working hard and working smart can sometimes be two different things

One of the important reasons why fixed jobs are not preferable for some people is because not all people are at their best at the same time of the day.

Some people are early risers who like working early in the day, while others might be night owls who like working during the night.

Whatever kind of person you may be, it is important to decide on a particular time of the day and follow it daily. Find the type of clothes you are most comfortable in, and start working without wasting any time.

Moreover, you need to find a place in your house where you can work properly without any distractions – this can also be outside your home, such as in a nearby cafe. In order to enhance productivity, you need to schedule your work effectively. Break down your work into small tasks and complete them accordingly.

3. Stay away from Distractions

It is crucial to make up your mind and stick with it.

Home can be filled with lot of distractions. Helping your sister with her daily chores or shopping with your neighbour can easily take away a lot of your time that can be spent on working.

At times, it is better to allocate some time for cleaning the house or doing the laundry (and all such types of chores). It is necessary to set some boundaries while working. Also, killing time on social media can be a major distraction. Playing a few more levels of Candy Crush on Facebook or tweeting about how you are feeling right now is not going to benefit you in any way.

Instead, set aside some time to engage yourself in social media so that it doesn't take up your valuable time while working. Stay away from these sites, or if possible, block them while working.

Learn to say 'NO' when needed, and in a convincing manner. At the same time. enjoy distractions if they're really unavoidable, as they can give you a break from your daily routine.

4. Separate work from personal life

Working from home is both awesome and frightening.

When you're working, do not let your personal life get in the way with your professional life. Reserve some time to be spent with your family and friends.

Meeting your friends during your work time can cause delay in completing the specific targets. Tell your friends in advance about your work timings so that they do not feel neglected.

Be clear about your working time. Allow yourself some free time, so that you do not overload yourself. Do things in your free time that you have always wanted to try.

Take up some new activity or cultivate a new hobby that will keep you engaged.

5. Take regular breaks

Sometimes a break from your routine is the very thing you need.

Working from home can at times be very tedious. If you don't maintain a fixed work schedule, you might become a workaholic, which will in turn affect your health. It's better if you take breaks at regular intervals so that it makes you feel fresh.

While in the office you interact with your colleagues and your staff, working alone might minimize the interactions. Go out as frequently as possible. Take a walk every evening or hit the gym, as it can give you the chance to interact with your friends and neighbours.

These are some of the basic tips you can follow to start working from you home. There is an endless list of suggestions and advices that you can easily get from your friends and family.

The major thing to consider is to not get disappointed, even if things don't work at the beginning. Have patience. Take a day off at times, and spend it doing things that you love the most. (This can give you energy in ways you never expected!)

Don't forget that your home also needs to be taken care of as much as your work.

So try to maintain a balance between the two, and it will lead to a happy life. Last but not least, don't look at past failures, ad instead, try focusing on your new goals and ambitions.

"Around here, however, we don't look backwards for very long. We keep moving forward, opening up new doors and doing new things, because we're curious...and curiosity keeps leading us down new paths." — Walt Disney Company

Chapter 7

Say Goodbye To Email Overload

Hard work spotlights the character of people: some turn up their sleeves, some turn

up their noses, and some don't turn up at all. **-Sam Ewing**

Fed up with seeing at least 10 new emails in your inbox on a daily basis? Yes, they are emails related to you (else they wouldn't have ended up in your in-box in the first place). But how much can you and your email accounts handle? Here are 5 simple tips to avoid email overload.

1. YOU MADE THE CHOICE!!

Let's face it. Half of those unwanted emails are ones you subscribed to, and in actuality, never opened. One good article doesn't ensure that your subscription to the site will bombard you with good articles. It just bombs and chokes your email with stuff that is in no way related to you. (Beware of sites that say subscription is free or a must.)

Even if you do end up subscribing to a particular site, double check their articles to confirm if you want to continue your subscription. I've tried creating a separate email address for these subscriptions, but in vain. (It still got overloaded).

You don't need to be notified for every click on your Facebook or Twitter account. Prioritise your notifications, or else, just disable them. If something's that important, you'll check for it without the notification.

2. SET AN EXAMPLE

The fewer emails you send, the fewer you tend to receive. This is one golden rule when it comes to emails. Be concise in your emails. Try finishing your niceties in the same email – not half a dozen emails to give your regards and to thank them for theirs. Avoid forwarding emails unless they absolutely have to be forwarded.

Turn off the "auto-invite friends" feature of any app that you are using. (Let's face it – half the emails are a dozen people inviting you to join the same site.)

3. FOLDERS TO HOLD THEM

Folders may be a Stone Age way of organizing emails, but they do it right every time. To have a dozen folders and end up with a clogged inbox is not doing it right. Before prioritising your mail, prioritise you folders. Do not end up creating a folder for every interest or topic.

The easiest and simplest way to organise your folders is to have a somewhat similar layout as the following: hurry (needs immediate action), deadlines (engagements having a week's deadline), filing (for future reference), clients, family, friends, e-shopping (for online shopping and related emails), and miscellaneous (related to your hobbies or other interests).

Few of these folders may not be applicable for most of you, so personalise according to your needs.

4. TIME TO UNCLOG WHAT'S LEFT

Now that you've reduced the number of emails you get and you've got them organised, how long do you plan on having them in your inbox? Just because you have a 15GB limit, doesn't mean you need to use it entirely.

Once a week, allot time to go through your emails and dispose those that simply sit in your mail. Yes, you've had a good laugh at that joke ,but it doesn't have to stay there forever. Coupons that expired weeks ago don't need to be there either.

Delete, archive or upload them into your cloud storage if it's that important (don't end up clogging that too).

5. APPS TO KEEP YOU HAPPY

It comes as a relief to find so many web-based applications to put us out of our misery. There are many out there, like *Boomerang, Alto, Sanebox, Mailbox, Unroll Me* and what not. While some are paid apps (*Sanebox*), most of them like *Alto* and *Unroll Me* are free. Here are two of my personal favourites:

Alto- The thing about this app besides being free is the great display and its user friendliness. *Alto* essentially categorises your emails based on pre-set patterns or the ones that you create. It moreover works through every email account of yours.

For example, you have daily deals and retailer stacks (for all those online shopping that we do). Stacks for a particular sender are also available. This works well for family or important clients.

Two of its important and most useful stacks are:

Photos stack - This pulls up any images that you get for your viewing. You can directly move them to other folders, download or share the photos. You can even sort the photos by sender, date or account. The interface alone is worth checking out.

Attachments stack - Tired of going through a dozen emails just to find that receipt from a week ago? Fret not – the attachments stack brings all your email attachments to a single stack and displays them via thumbnails. These can also be sorted by sender, date and account.

You can also create stacks for topics of your interest in a simple drag-and-drop manner. The only drawback is the current absence of a mobile version of this app.

Unroll Me - If you don't want to focus on the organising part, but rather the actual load shedding part, this is the app for you. It routinely checks through your subscription emails and presents you with only one subscription email per day.

Finding your previous email-of-the-day is no big deal, as it's stored in the archive; you can also get a sneak peek of the one you will receive the day after. One incredibly good feature of this app is that unsubscribing is just a click away (even if an unsubscribe link isn't available).

This app also allows you to block contacts who keep spamming you. The good thing is, there is no limit on the number of contacts or senders whom you can block. This app also overcomes the drawback of *Alto* by having a mobile version that's extremely easy to use.

Here's to a cleaner inbox. But just remember, you can always follow one simple and easy tip to avoid this altogether - don't hand out your email address that easily.

Chapter 8

Why You Must Join a Mastermind Group

I've learned from experience that if you work harder at it, and apply more energy and time to it, and more consistency, you get a better result. It comes from the work.
-Louis C. K.

Chris Guillebeau once said "If Plan A does not seem to work, there are 25 letters to follow." Brainstorming for ideas is tough, and finding solutions for problems is even tougher. Often, we feel like we're up against a wall. Sometimes, the best way to deal with problems is to discuss them.

Seventy-five years ago, Napoleon Hill in his book, "Think and Grow Rich," introduced the concept of Mastermind Groups. These groups usually have a minimum of 6 members, and they meet in stipulated times to discuss and overcome problems.

This isn't your typical therapy group; these groups operate on utmost professionalism. Brainstorming, listening, and problem-solving are just some of the functions of the group.

1. Not your average problem-solving session:

In management textbooks, over 26 idea generation techniques are listed, from methods of note-taking to the famous Taguchi Method. Problems arise everywhere. Mastermind Groups, however, help in making sure your problems are heard. Also, you get to hear perspectives from like-minded people in your profession. This way, you are forced to take a step back and listen to new solutions. One might even be helpful to you.

Since Mastermind Groups meet once a week, they usually have an agenda for each meeting. For example, one particular topic might be addressed in every meeting. Or, the meetings can be person-centric. Mastermind Groups usually have members belonging to the same profession. There may be people who have already encountered these problems. So, finding a solution isn't that tough.

2. Building and expanding your network:

Mastermind Groups have anywhere between 6 to 20 members. The members meet once a week, and they may be from the same profession, but they are usually from diverse backgrounds. For every problem discussed, you might have an interesting solution.

Furthermore, while you have problems, there might be people to help you. Furthermore, they might be interested in collaborating and working with you. They might have some resource or idea to add on to your existing database.

Don't be afraid of meeting the wrong people. Most Mastermind Groups have a process of admitting members. Some prefer a formal or informal interview, while others may have application forms.

Since knowledge and experience are vital, these group need to ensure that members are of a certain caliber. The reason behind this is simple: the others require you, as much as you require them.

Going to work for a large company is like getting on a train. Are you going sixty miles an hour or is the train going sixty miles an hour and you're just sitting still? - **J. Paul Getty**

Mastermind Groups are mostly started online, and you can find them with the click of a button. Before you go ahead and look for one, make sure that you ready to open up to a group. In these groups, no negative remarks or criticisms are exchanged. One person is pre-determined to present a problem each week.

3. Brainstorming beyond ideas:

Mastermind Groups are created for every profession out there, literally. Although originally started for businesses, there are blogging Mastermind Groups and animation Mastermind Groups.

These groups all serve the purpose of solving tough problems. They bounce ideas off each other, get new ideas, and in a way, grow together. And growing with a community of like-minded people is both rewarding and satisfying. Some groups recite their problems in an orderly fashion, so each one can be solved.

Many bloggers have reported that these groups are extremely insightful and helpful. Addressing your problems to people helps you take a step back and review your problem objectively. When you think of your problems in this manner, accepting ideas and thinking out-of-the box come right your way.

4. Go online and participate:

One of the key ideas for starting such groups is participation. To join a Mastermind Group, you can search online or browse on Facebook, as many have Facebook pages for themselves. Another way to find a Mastermind Group nearby is to go on Craigslist or meetup.com. These places play host to a lot of such groups.

Sometimes, these groups are more active over the web - they connect through video chats and hangouts. Moreover, they have events like conferences, apart from regular group meetings. The meetings can be both formal and informal, depending on the group.

Sometimes, there's a beginning, middle and end to each meeting. The "beginning" involves each member reflecting on goals they set the previous week. They also speak about their progress towards achieving these goals. The "middle" is the part of the meeting where one person addresses his or her problems.

The "end"" is when the members offer solutions and ideas to tackle the problems. By the end of the meeting, each member sets a certain number of goals that they would like to achieve before the next meeting.

5. Finding the true meaning of team work:

As an employee, blogger or businessman, you probably feel lost and alone at the face of a problem. Often, what someone needs when facing a problem is numerous people racking their brains together to find a solution. However, the concept of "team-work" is hardly seen anywhere these days.

Mastermind Groups can prove you wrong. The premise of starting a group like this is to help people get together, learn and then grow. They believe in problem-solving through a collective approach.

The members collaborate within themselves and help out as much as possible. Since everyone is from a similar profession, the advice thrown around can be extremely useful. The more you work together, the more you can achieve.

In fact, what you get by joining a group like this is business advisors. Since these people know the loops of the job, they will able to guide you through tough times. The process of learning to solve problem with a group of people is wholesome. You can take away these techniques and implement them in your business as well.

In short, the levels of satisfaction from members across the world are extraordinary.

Joining a group like this is like getting access to an exclusive community – a place where one can think, learn and grow. All this is done in a sustainable and healthy way.

Mastermind Groups embrace the true meaning of a community by being a force that works together. And at the end of the day, everyone stands to gain.

Chapter 9

Let's Make Those Boring Meetings more Productive

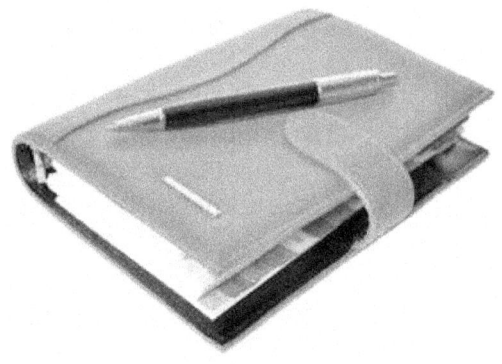

There is always the danger that we may just do the work for the sake of the work. This is where the respect and the love and the devotion come in - that we do it to God, to Christ, and that's why we try to do it as beautifully as possible. -**Mother Teresa**

Does the word 'meeting' drain all your energy? No, meetings do not have to be boring at all!

Meetings enable you to come up with creative ideas and share them with others; they are a form of social interaction. Here are 5 tips to make meetings more productive.

1. Invite the right people

For a meeting to be productive, you've got to invite the right people. Inviting too many people will make it hard for you to hear each person's opinion individually.

Also, inviting a bunch of wrong people can be less productive than having one-on-one meetings, so invite people who can help you reach the goals of the meeting. You can use the Doodle software to create polls and suggest the dates and time to the members of the meeting to find out what time they are comfortable with.

Choose the right person to lead the meeting, as a meeting without a person to lead it may run to risk of becoming chaotic and ultimately unproductive. If a leader is not chosen, a dominating person might take over, which might be irritating.

2. Organize the meeting

Prepare an agenda for the meeting, and mail it beforehand to the participants. This will help them prepare their thoughts and ideas before the meeting. Allot some time for the agenda and stick to it.

This will avoid boredom or frustration from setting in. Instead of having the meeting for an hour, have irregular time intervals like 20 minutes or 35 minutes. This will help them stay focused. Or ask one member in the meeting to keep track of the time and to give signals when the discussion exceeds the time allotted; this guarantees that the meeting is short and structured.

Never allow late-comers; they will take time to settle in after causing noisy distractions and will ask for an update, which will disrupt the flow of the meeting.

Meetings – especially the ones attended by a lot of people – tend to get delayed. Colleagues might want to chat about their own personal lives. In that case, ask them to come early. A meeting that starts late will end late. This will make them impatient, and the meeting will not have the desired outcome.

And to end the meeting on time, book other appointments after the meeting. So when you start the meeting you can tell the participants that you have an appointment right

after the meeting that you can't afford to miss.
Ban smartphones and laptops during the meetings so that they don't check e-mails or use Twitter or Facebook.

When people return from the break, have them switch their seats. This will take them out of their comfort zone and will force them into listening. Lesser known fact, but really effective! Having heavy meals and unhealthy foods during lunchtime meetings can make people sluggish. Instead, give them healthy, protein-packed foods, which will boost their energy.

3. Prepare yourself

Set the goals you want to achieve from the meeting. The purpose of the meeting may be to solve a problem, to make decisions or to share information. This forms the basis of your agenda. With everyone behind their laptops, it might be hard to continuously watch the leader of the meeting.

So it is necessary for the leader to keep moving around and be dynamic during the meeting. Interact with all the members and involve them in the discussion.

Some people will shoot out their opinion and some will just make faces, so make sure to read their expressions and ask for their opinion if they have one. Ask everyone to take part in the meeting by giving their comments and feedback. Take notes when people come up with points. Prevent the discussion from going off-topic. Organize points and topics on a flipboard or a white-board to keep track of your agenda.

At the end of the meeting, summarize all the points. This will allow you to easily come to a conclusion as to what the out-come of the meeting is. After the meeting, send feedback notes. This will make the participants feel that they have done some-thing productive and encourage them to contribute more next time.

Also, compile the notes and send the follow-up to the members after the meeting. Make a list of what action items have to be done by whom to give them a clear idea of what has to be done.

4. Go online

It is better to host an online meeting than to travel around the world. This saves you time, hotel charges and travel costs. Use ef-ficient software tools to hold the meeting.

Stay away from software that require down-loads. Some software may trip you up on system requirements. Choose software that are easy to use. You can even record these meetings and send it to those who were not able to make it to the meeting.

5. Presentations

Talking continuously for hours can make your co-workers to start daydreaming. To hold onto their attention, show them some PowerPoint presentations. The slides should have just the key points, listed in bullets. Do not paste long paragraphs onto the slides; nobody's going to have the pa-tience to read them. If you want to talk to people about a product, show them the live demo of the product rather than its pictures or videos.

Moreover, no machine can be trusted, so be sure to have a backup of the presentation in a pen drive. Or, if you have the presentation saved in a cloud service, you can simply switch to another machine. If you don't have a backup and if something goes wrong with the presentation, it will bring down the confidence others have in you. It will also bring down your own self-confidence.

Rehearse what you're going to say and check if it fits within the specified time. Set up the presentation and check if everything is okay a few minutes before the meeting starts.

By following these tips, you can make your co-workers more enthusiastic. This will increase the productivity of the company. The employees will feel more productive and more satisfied.

So plan the agenda well and see your organization grow. Good luck!

Chapter 10

5 Secrets to Work Like a Ninja and Save Time

Luck? I don't know anything about luck. I've never banked on it and I'm afraid of people who do. Luck to me is something

else: Hard work - and realizing what is opportunity and what isn't. **-Lucille Ball**

Ever had problems managing deadlines or handling multiple tasks? Often, in today's money-minded world, we want work to be perfect and delivered on time.

In a quest to make work more fruitful, profitable, and precise, we sometimes lose ourselves in the whirlpool of perfection and preciseness and miss our deadlines; ultimately, all our highly devoted efforts go unrewarded.

No matter how hard you try recovering and rebuilding your skills, you still are unable to match tables all around, and you're left with more frustration and less productivity.

So, there's definitely something you're missing out in your endeavour to make your work efficient and effective.

Below are 5 tips to achieve definite success:

1. Prioritize:

Often, we are loaded with a lot of work, and when it comes to delivering, we're all in a willy-nilly state. It then becomes very difficult and almost impossible to differentiate what's important and what isn't. At that eleventh hour, we tend to muddle up and adulterate all of the work, and ultimately, nothing works out. All tasks seem to be important, and the outcome is nothing but a conundrum.

Often what makes most of us lag in our work is doing the job that we like the most, instead of doing the job that needs to be done first. This not only makes us miss important tasks, but also breeds in us the tendency to avoid tasks that are urgent.

A man's work is nothing but this slow trek to rediscover, through the detours of art, those two or three great and simple images in whose presence his heart first opened. -**Albert Camus**

I will give a perfect formula to ease you out of this lose-lose situation and convert it into a win-win one. An elixir by Charles Hummel brings us out of this mess. Hummel suggests taking the list of things you need to do and dividing the tasks based on urgency and important.

Firstly, list all your tasks on a piece of paper.

Secondly, categorize each task into one of four of the following categories.

Important and Urgent	Important and Non Urgent
Unimportant and Urgent	Unimportant and Non Urgent

This organizes your to-do list, and you can now do the important and urgent things at first go, and leave your unimportant and non-urgent jobs to the end. This process not only saves time, but also results in a more effective, efficient, and stress-free lifestyle.

2. Focus:

The next tip is to focus on the job that we have planned to work on. Already, the priority chart has helped us identify the tasks that need the utmost attention. Next is focusing on that one particular task we aim to achieve.

These are a list of things that will help you achieve focus:

Determination

A strong will power is required to maintain your focus on one task. This determination to complete is something you should strive to keep and strengthen.

Turn off notifications, pop-ups and wireless devices.

In this world of gizmos, it may be difficult to cut off from all the electronic gadgets we're surrounded with; however, eliminating these distractions will certainly help sharpen your focus.

<u>Organize your workspace</u>

No one likes to work in a clouded frame of mind or an unorganized mess. Consider these two working environments, where one is well kempt, lively and organized, and the other shabby, chaotic and muddled up with a legion of unwanted stuffs. Without any second thought, I believe you'd prefer the cleaner and more organized space.

Don't you then agree that once your workplace is all nicely tidied up and well placed, your concentration will improve? So, liven up your room with enough light and organize your work space.

<u>Meditate</u>

And the last method to sharpen your focus is to keep yourself calm. You can achieve a sense of calm through various techniques, but the one truly effective way is through meditation. You need not go to the Himalayas to find your peace of mind; instead, devoting 10-20 minutes a day in your own place can help improve your concentration and focus.

Keep your mind calm and find a silent place to medicate. Usually, the morning hours are a peaceful time for most people, but any quiet time during the day is suitable.

Stop thinking of your problems, work, deadlines, commitments and all worldly problems for once. Concentrate only on your mind and gradually your body. Think of relaxing and positive things.

Keep your eyes closed while meditating, as it cuts off the contact with the physical world. Rub your palms together and let the warmth of them touch your eyes while opening them.

3. Assortment and Break Down:

Another important and easy way to work on your task is the way you proceed to complete it. It is important for you to sort out the way you plan, outline, and structure your workflow.

This helps in dividing your work into smaller and simpler assignments, breaking down your big problem into smaller, more manageable tasks.

Confronting one big project is usually stressful, but completing smaller tasks seems less daunting. This encourages you stay relaxed and energized, allowing you to face the next big project with enthusiasm and energy.
Putting it in Peter Marshall's words, *"Small deeds done are better than great deeds planned"*. So, accomplish the impossible by breaking it down into smaller tasks.

4. Take Breaks:

After achieving the small tasks, relish and enjoy your victory. Pat yourself on the back and congratulate every small achievement. This indefinitely keeps you motivated and enthusiastic.

You can take a walk away from your workplace, sip a coffee, and listen to soothing songs that make you feel confident and driven. A little bit of stretching, looking out of your window, having a little chat with your colleagues or friends could do the charm. Plan your break on a regular basis, although taking too many breaks may make you stray from your work and lose focus.

So, cherish your small victories but plan the breaks out.

5. Enjoy the work:

No matter how much you prioritize, focus, or divide, it is actually the passion for your work that should drive you. That feeling of positivity or optimism has to be engrained within you. You should feel it, realize it and use it to enjoy your work.

This feeling drives you to love your work no matter how ugly it might get. So, do not carry anything negative in your thoughts, and strive to always feel an aura of freshness and positivity around you to achieve your goals.

Chapter 11

Brainstorm Ideas like Einstein

The brain is a wonderful organ; it starts working the moment you get up in the

morning and does not stop until you get into the office. **-Robert Frost**

Brainstorming is an effective tool for creativity. It has seen a sharp rise in its use to generate creative ideas all around the world, and it has struck a chord with people from all walks of life.

From freelance writers, journalists, novelists to industrial giants, everyone seems to be brainstorming to create and keep the work flow going.

Brainstorming is useful wherever cognitive ideating is required.

And if small businesspeople say they made it on their own, all they are saying is that nobody else worked seven days a week in their place. Nobody showed up in their place to open the door at five in the morning. Nobody did their thinking, and worrying, and sweating for them. **-Paul Ryan**

It is a gem of a tool that helps 'ideation'. This is the reason contemporary authors and writers have taken up this method of honing their skills of creation.

It is an act of gathering all the latent, hidden ideas from your subconscious. You do this by seeing, thinking, visualizing and letting your thoughts run wild.

Continue the processes until you have a list of ideas, from which you can choose relevant points. It is practiced individually or in a group; this depends on the type of the issue and the number of people affected by it. Brainstorming is the means in itself and not the end.

Here are a few useful tips to chisel your brainstorming skills:

1. Locate the root of your 'exact problem':

You need to know the exact problem to find the proper solution. By 'exact problem', what's meant is that you should not have a vague idea of the issue, but you should be able to highlight the exact issue.

A problem is always multilateral. The triggering point of a problem is different than the stage you might be in, so you need to locate the stage of the problem you are in. This is an easy thing to do. One can achieve this by the method of simple deduction.

You need to strike out the elements of the problem that might not be of concern to you. Keep going until you reach a point when you come to know your exact problem.

2. Watch, Think and Visualize:

Once you are at the root of the problem, the actual brain work starts. This is the point at which you start to think of ways to solve the problem.

Three simple ways will help you facilitate this process. **Try watching things** around you – anything and everything – as it helps the mind run free. Do not just see but watch, and try to find something that might relate to your problem at hand. If you find anything at all, make a note of it.

Then **try flexing your brain** muscles by thinking about anything that might prove to be a solution. Think until your brain gets tired. Again, make note of whatever your mind produces in the process.

Another effective means is to **visualize.** Visualizing includes stirring up your subconscious mind, which helps you to search your 'mind palace' to find something that you might have experienced, learnt, seen or read in the past that might be helpful in the present situation. Don't forget to take notes.

3. Never reject an idea or a thought:

Remember, every thought is precious at this point. You need to respect the uniqueness of an idea. Make a note of anything that comes to the mind. This is what we call free-writing.

Don't try to edit while you think. Let your thoughts flow as freely as they can. You can choose and discard later on when you have completed your brainstorming session.

4. Reorganize the data collected in the process:

Now it is time to manage what you have done. Gather all the data that you have produced during the process and organize and reorganize until you feel that it is making some sense.

To do this, you simply have to collect all the notes you've made and categorize them. Rewrite them while you divide your notes into different categories, perhaps based on similarity of the points, or their respective relativity to the problem.

Once you have organized your thoughts, you are ready for the final act.

5. Review, choose and create:

Once you pen down your thoughts and organize them, you are free to review them. Then choose whatever you feel is relevant to your problem and discard the unwanted stuff. This act is the last step you take before you find the solution. In the notes that you make from your random thoughts, you will find at least a hint, if not more.

Somewhere in your thoughts, you will find an opened door, which will mark a fresh start. The point here is that the door has always existed; you only changed the angle of looking at your problem, and after you did this, you were able to find it. And now that you have found it, you are on your path of creation again.

The act of brainstorming is the mental equivalent to exercising your body. It takes some effort, but it produces results. You should always remember and trust one thing: your brain is the most fascinating and intriguing asset you have. It has the power to create and destroy at will.

When you channel your stream of thoughts in the right direction, you witness the miracles. It is your brain and the way you let it work that define your being. Brainstorming is ideating and meditating at the same time. It takes you to different places while you are sitting on the couch in your living room.

On the other hand, it also helps you to learn from your past experiences and use them to find solutions to problems in the present.

Idea brainstorming, despite being a modern concept, has helped many; enthusiasts around the world practice it with ease.

So now it is your turn to give it a try. Trust in it and keep trying until you see the difference for yourself.

It might take some time, but if you practice it with a positive mind, it will certainly be of immense help to you.

Chapter 12

Tackle the Humongous Workload like A Zen Master

Work is love made visible. And if you cannot work with love but only with distaste, it is better that you should leave your work and sit at the gate of the temple and take alms of those who work with joy. **-Khalil Gibran**

"Targets, Competition, Pay hike, Work load and so on." Every working professional today is mulling over these words day and night.

Time has become expensive, owing to the unscrupulous amount of work being loaded onto people. This also causes a build-up of stress and fear of failure among the employees in an organization. No wonder human resources departments are increasingly facing the challenge of employee retention.

The companies cannot be blamed, as they are only trying to sustain themselves; however, in this rat race of sustenance and grabbing market share, the employees are being overworked. So to help these employees, here are a few tips and precautions to be taken when the work becomes excessive.

1. Highlight Priorities

We tend to shuffle our projects, especially when we have a lot of them, but this practice needs to be ended. Whenever you are assigned a task, take time and analyze its importance.

Make a list of all the tasks at hand and rate them on a scale of one to ten based on their importance, and write down this number next to each task. This will help in identifying the most urgent tasks that require your immediate attention.

Focus on them and stop worrying about others. When you prioritize your projects, half the battle is won. Thereafter, you just need to plan their execution and implement it.

2. Seek help and delegate

Often times, managers do not want to share their responsibilities, even when they are unable to handle them. My friend! The earth won't fall apart if you try to ask for help from your colleagues, nor will your self-respect be diminished.

Instead, you will be able to reap many benefits. One, you will have less burden and will be able to focus on your prioritized tasks. Second, you may have never thought of doing the work in the manner your colleague suggests. Perhaps it proves to be a better bet. This will also boost your confidence, as you will be sure of the reliability of the other person.

This works in a mind boggling corporate culture. You have to make your way to get your work done there. The only solution to this is, 'Help and Seek help.'

3. Dictate deadlines and adhere to them

Be a little stubborn with this. Time yourself while doing a particular job, but while doing this, do not tax yourself too much. Save time for breaks.

In short, make a realistic timetable. If you have assigned a part of your work to someone else, make sure that the person does it on time. Do not postpone when you have made a decision.

Learn to value the importance of time, and you shall never fail. Even when the project results are not as expected, do not waste time regretting it. If you think that it can be rectified, do it. Or else, leave it.

Even when you are free, persuade yourself to devise a better way of completing the task. When you complete your task in time, this gives you the motivation to get onto other projects with vigor and enthusiasm.

4. 'No' can save your life

Literally! This is not the era in which your boss's command is final. Now, you have the right to stand up and refuse to take up a project. Hey, wait! Before taking this step, you need to have a reason to say no.

First, let your brain run over the whole scenario. If you have no other or only a small amount of projects at hand, please, take it. If you think that this project can earn you a good place in the eyes of management, you are advised to grab it, regardless of how complicated the it may be. Do not miss any opportunity that may prove to be good for your career.

However, if you know that this task is too much or may negatively impact your performance, it is better that you say "No." At least, for once, your boss needs to understand that you are not a machine. She or he will surely contemplate before giving you another such task. Also, when your colleagues keep asking you time and again to help them out, do not feel guilty to say "No."

5. Avoid being a perfectionist

Nobody is perfect. You need to bear this in mind. Some may like your work, others may not. You cannot please everyone. So when your task is rated 'A,' do not get upset over the fact that you didn't get an 'A+'. That sense of being a perfectionist drives you away from your deadlines, which is a blunder.

You need to understand that all that matters is productivity. To understand this better, let us look at an example. Mr. Paul and Mr. Russell work as relationship managers in one of the leading banks.

Initially, they both had twenty clients each. Recently, in a meeting, it came to the notice of the management that Mr. Paul has managed to attract six more customers. All his clients are quite happy with him. Mr. Russell's clients are very happy with his services, but he has never had over twenty clients. Naturally, Mr. Paul becomes the favorite employee. Despite being very good, Mr. Russell could not impress management.

This is, because he was doing what he was expected to do. Mr. Paul did something that the management never thought he would be able to do. He did this by doing his job sincerely and smartly. He avoided being a perfectionist.

Work is worship, no doubt, but you must keep your eyes and ears open while you work. Tactful attitude is the only key way that can make you productive despite the mounting workload.

The new generation is smarter. You need to be balanced to cope with the increasing demands. These tips are tried and tested by many professionals. Hope this helps you too.

Chapter 13

Spice Up Your Work Environment

Every man's work, whether it be literature, or music or pictures or architecture or anything else, is always a portrait of himself. -**Samuel Butler**

Stability is something that we are constantly trying to achieve in our lives, whether in our career or personal lives.

But then, why are individuals juggling between jobs so often? Is it the boredom of a single job that creeps inside after every couple of years, or is it the luring hikes in that other company?

Whatever it is, let's for now stop worrying and aim towards enhancing our productivity. So tomorrow, when you sit at your desk, keep these tips in mind.

1. Pop up with playful ideas

Enough of being so stubborn, and save yourself from being a fatso sitting in front of the screen making spreadsheets. If nothing else, at least play with your computer. Wait!

By this, I don't mean play games on your computer. In fact, what I am trying to till in your head is that you can try to beautify your work by making it look pleasing to the eyes.

For example, Mr. Gerard never presents without making his presentation appear good and appealing. He makes sure that he has used the right combination of colors and fonts in his Power Point. He does this when he is utterly tired of analyzing spread-sheets. Even in Excel, he makes proper charts and presents his work neatly.

Isn't that an amazing exercise? He is having fun playing with the colors, tables, pictures and chats, while simultaneously enhancing his presentation. Work becomes fun and inviting.

2. Crave to be better than the best

Whenever you are assigned a project, try to find out who has done a similar project ear-lier and who has done it the right way. Now, instead of copying the same, strain your brains and set yourself a benchmark.

Referring to projects done before will help you save time, which you can use for your own project. Try doing it after you have mapped your plans for the project so that your baby ideas (which might be better) are not nipped. After analyzing the prospects, create your new game plan and beat the bull.

Never show your good things at one go. Keep doing that in bits and parts. Do not make the best presentation on day 1. If you know the technicalities of your work, it's always better to amaze people bit by bit. Expectations grow, and your boss may assume you will exceed his or her expectations every time, judging you with higher standards.

3. Make your own style steadily

One's style of handling a situation makes his unique identity in every workplace. If you are the boss, would you send a short tempered person to a client? Or would you allow a gossip monger employee to manage the staff when you are away? No.

Everyone prefers to work with someone who is reliable and pleasing. The way you dress, talk and balance your emotions is your style. People notice it every time, even when you are having a light time in the office party.

So keep watch on your activities. Be natural. At the same time, let everyone realize your presence and respect you, in style!

4. Bar the monotony and negativity

One thing you should never forget is, 'You are hired, because you are good and you will succeed, because you are improving.'

A) Write this line on a sticky note.
B) Highlight the word 'improving'
C) Now, stick it on your desk.

Mood swings can make you depressed at times. But hey! That's human. Relax! Even if you didn't succeed this time, you still have the ability to achieve your goal. It may take time, but never sit and cry or mentally blame yourself. Instead, keep a strong heart.

Try again and again and again until you achieve your goal, because that sense of achievement will drive you further. If someone ridicules you or makes fun of you, ignore it for the time being; they will regret it later. So never let your pace slow in any situation, whether good or not.

If still, you have not been able to get over your trauma, just get up and fetch a 1st Class student's English book. Read the story "Edison's light bulb" at least 20 times.

5. End with a treat

Now! For all your hard work and brain-storming, celebrate your success with yourself. Although completing the work and being recognized is in itself a grace, go out and treat yourself the way you want. Stop!

What about those colleagues and your boss who helped you throughout the project, who believed in you even when you were apprehensive about yourself? You owe them for their help, so send a thank you email or a card, or go and personally appreciate their role in your project. Whenever you get a chance, appreciate them in front of others. This assures them that you value their suggestions.

Party, shop, eat and laugh your heart out. This will revitalize your energy and prepare you for the challenges ahead. Spend time to introspect yourself and thank God for His blessings on you. Share your experiences with others.

We have grown up playing 'Office Office,' wishing that we will be happier when we grow up and start working. Re-kindle that dream and live it to the fullest by making your workplace productive and pleasing and you will never have to look for work at a new place. All the best!

Chapter 14

The Time Bandit Solution

Once you start a working on something, don't be afraid of failure and don't abandon it. People who work sincerely are the happiest. **–Chanakya**

Time is the only standard that is universal. Even currencies have different values, but time does not. With a stature that high, it is easy to say that we take it for granted.

When we were children, we put off chores. As college students, we turned our assignments in late. In the office, we pile work up and break our heads over it at the last minute.

Stolen time is as good as gone; we can ever get it back. However, what we can do is rectify ourselves. Time management is crucial at any stage of life, and here are some tips that might just save the day:

1. An opportunity is one that is seized:

Most successful entrepreneurs have one advice: do not postpone your work.

Time isn't qualitative; it is a force so strong that almost everything is measured by it. When you have a target set in front of you, you adhere to it. When speaking of time-wasting tactics, it extends to all age groups.

Before exams, students find umpteen reasons to distract themselves. In the workplace, we lose valuable time on social networking sites. Sometimes, even watching paint dry seems fun compared to the work we know we have to do.

When we speak of stolen time, we should realize that it has more than just one ill effect, such as laziness, procrastination and an idle mind. What one should understand is that time-wasting becomes a habit after a while. It is lecherous and drags you down.

Before you know it, you won't be doing much work; you'll be turning in assignments late. At the end of the day, you don't get work done.

Sooner or later, you will just be another demotivated person, filled with regret.

The first tip is to raise your hand up high, and say "I WILL DO IT." Even if you realize that you have wasted time earlier, work now.

The human mind is extremely powerful, and two hours of concentration could take you places.

"Procrastination is deadly, the present is now. And now is the best time."

Write that down, and keep repeating it every time you find yourself looking elsewhere while trying to finish a task.

2. The social media menace:

A study from a leading science magazine concluded that an average person checks Facebook over 14 times a day. This number increases when they have to do more work. After all, we like to take breaks.

Think about this question: are we taking a break from work to check social media, or is it the other way around?
Addiction to social media is dangerous for personal productivity. It does not matter how often you check your social feeds; when you have a report due the next day, wasting any time is hazardous to your abilities and the productivity of the organization.

Set a limit. It could be a time-based one, or a work-based one; what matters is that you follow it strictly. It will be tough in the beginning, since you are so used to being "connected". Your palms might even itch to see the friend requests you've gotten.

Get over that. Being addicted to anything is bad, and the internet virus can potentially be fatal to your work life. There are websites that can help you count down time, so you can go back to doing work.

When work is concerned, make sure you have a single-track mind. Finish the job and everyone's happy. Social media will always be around, but lost time won't.

3. Chart it out:

Studies show that time-wasting is usually a result of no planning.

When a project sits in front of you, spend time thinking about how you are going to approach it. Most of the time, cluelessness leads to boredom. When you are bored, you look for things to distract you. There again, you find yourself losing time.

What you need to do is prioritize. Spend ten minutes every day organizing your daily tasks. This way, you have a rough idea as to how to spend your time usefully. Further, you can plan your breaks without stressing out about deadlines. When you plan this way, you are less prone to wasting time. You'll be able to master your day and know what is lined up in front of you.

This act of planning keeps you flexible, stimulated and extremely productive.

4. De-clutter procrastination:

Procrastination has been mentioned, but it deserves a special headline.

When you stare out of the window, or play Angry Birds on your phone, that's procrastination. Although procrastination is putting "off" work, there is one kind that is silent and deadly – the kind where you have an important task waiting in front of you, and you ignore it.

Instead, you focus on doing menial tasks given to you. When you prioritize less important tasks, you are going backwards. Goals should always be in descending order of importance.

Here are some ways to help you out:
-Make your daily to-do list in order of priority. This makes you more disciplined. Plus, all the tough jobs are done earlier in the day, when you likely have more energy.

-Use time management software, such as Time Boxing. This way, you can comprehensively set alarms, make checklists and schedule tasks.

- Scheduling your tasks and being mindful of the time will give you a sense of alertness. Also, instructions are much clearer, and you don't waste time.

5. The end isn't easy to reach:

This is the hardest tip yet. When you've built up the habit of wasting time, it's hard to get out of it; bad habits take years to form, so you can't just demolish them in seconds.
Make sure that you devote some time every day to pamper yourself with the objects of distraction. This way, you aren't being hard on yourself, but you are slowly overcoming these obstacles.

Managing time isn't tough if you set your duties aside from leisure. Often, the two are mixed together, and this is where all the confusion comes from.

When your mind is calm and focused, time will be on your side, and so will your work.

Chapter 15

So Much paper, So less Time !

For me, every day is a new thing. I approach each project with a new insecurity, almost like the first project I ever did. And I get the sweats. I go in and start working, I'm not sure where I'm going. If I knew

where I was going I wouldn't do it. **-Frank Gehry**

The importance of managing time cannot be emphasised enough.
It doesn't matter if you're a student or a businessman; the skill to manage time is one of utmost importance, however rarely found.

Most internet posts will give you some of the most common ways to improve your time management skills along with the reasons to follow them.

It is essential for you to know though, that very few of them, if any, actually work.

Most of them need you to modify your life and change routines that you've been following since a long time. It is usually impractical and therefore, not applicable to most people.

So what are the easier ways to go about this?

Well, here are some which will not need you to make any major changes in your lifestyle. So here you go!

1. Using your unproductive time for planning purposes

Umberto Eco, the essayist, novelist and se-miotician, after he wrote his ground-breaking metaphysical novel, 'The name of The Rose', was asked how he gets so much work done.

Eco has written more than 50 books (including novels, non-fiction books and the like). His reply to the question was intriguing. He said that he never wasted a single moment.

Even at times when he would be waiting for the elevator, or taking a bath, he would think of his next piece of work.
He would use the most unproductive of moments to plan, think of stories, plots and ideas.

So try making the best use of your low time, which are times when you go for a bath, prepare food, eat, brush or wait for some-one.

Try planning, making mental lists (or real ones), analyse mentally and get these cognition-based tasks out of the way in these moments.

2. Plan your breaks

If you have ever taken study breaks during exams in your school days, you will know the importance of planning them.

Likewise, when you have work to do and goals to reach, you cannot waste too much time on breaks. Plan your breaks according to your workload and stress/energy levels. Don't take more than 10-15 minutes off after every couple of hours and in this time, think of things that are not related to the work you are doing.

Another thing to keep in mind is that during these breaks, don't do things that will distract you too much - like watching TV or using social media. Get a snack or have a small chat with your family. You can also listen to a couple of songs you like, but remember- only a couple! Music can also be extremely distracting.

3. Organise yourself beforehand

Set up your work area in a way that the first thing you do when you start work is NOT looking for things or cleaning up.

Make To-Do lists for the next day in advance before closing work. This way, when you start work the next day, you do not have excuses to procrastinate by setting up or planning etc.

A piece of advice though - try making these plans only a day in advance. A timetable made a week ago or a planner kept since a long time doesn't really work. If the plans are fresh, they remain in your mind and you will not be in for a surprise.

4. Eliminate all sorts of distractions

Well, distractions only work when you want to get distracted, and in that case, anything can become a distraction.

However, try eliminating the most common distractions. My colleagues usually prefer switching off their phones and go offline of social media sites. Just like in schools or colleges you are often asked to turn your phones off and only the websites that are relevant to the work/course are allowed access to.

Likewise, don't open any webpages/links that are not relevant to the work you are doing. Also, don't answer the phone and switch the answering machine on.

You can also ask your family/friends/colleagues to leave you alone when you're working to further cut down on distractions. Try to meet lesser people and attend only those meetings which are important and that don't make you compromise on the work front.

If you are easily distracted, try isolating your workspace. Work in a space that helps you concentrate on the work you are doing.

Have a formal setting, tables and proper chairs instead of couches or anything too comfortable (like recliners, beds or bean bags). You can also have a corresponding break-room, where you can have snacks, music, books etc. that you can indulge in during your mini-breaks.

5. Personal deadlines and focus

Avoid multi-tasking and focus on one task at a time. Do the important ones at the beginning. Likewise, do the smaller, easier and quicker tasks first so that you can focus your complete attention on the bigger, more time-consuming tasks later.

Try having personal deadlines for each task. My mother's sister, for example, who is a teacher and home-maker, uses this formula.

She usually devotes an hour to herself after school, then an hour for cooking.

Then she devotes two-three hours for doing jobs like correcting exam scripts and making teaching plans, an hour for cleaning the house.

To fulfill a dream, to be allowed to sweat over lonely labor, to be given a chance to create, is the meat and potatoes of life. The money is the gravy. - **Bette Davis**

This way, all your work gets done on time. I used to manage time like this in school, preparing for exams. I would give more hours to the bigger assignments and do them at the end.

Time management is not really as easy as it is made to sound.

However, it is also not extremely difficult. Once you start using these methods as part of your daily routine, you will be able to cut time wastage and get work done a lot more easily.

You will also save a lot of time to indulge in leisure activities, get some time alone, or even get to spend quality time with your family/friends. Managing time will help you finish work faster and increase your productivity. And what's more?

It will also reduce stress, and since you will have extra time, the quality of your product will improve massively as you will not have sub-standard work done in haste.

Thus, it can help you in a lot more ways than you'd think!

Conclusion

Thank you once again for buying this book. I have tried to be as precise as possible with this little book. I hope it was worth your time.

Procrastination affects every one of us. To become more productive, we need to work on it everyday.

By following the techniques that are outlined in this book, you will soon become free from the grasp of inefficiency.

Try to implement atleast 3 things mention in this book today. Get on to it right now. It's your first step towards productivity.

I will conclude it by saying, "Thoughts are useless without putting them into actions".

I want to connect with my readers on a personal level. Although, I charge for my consultation, I want to offer a **FREE** consultancy to my first 50 readers. You can ask me any question related to your life. Here's the form: http://bit.ly/askjoemartin

Please Review It On Amazon

Finally, if you have enjoyed reading this book and have benefited from it, please take the time to **post a review** and share your thoughts **on Amazon**. I will be very obliged, and it would be hugely appreciated. I want to help people and change their lives, and you can enable me to do that by simply sharing an honest review of this book, so that it can reach many more people.

If you aren't happy about this book or have any feedback, then please send me an email directly at joemartin-book@yahoo.com. I am committed to improving this book and making it as profound as possible, so that it can benefit more people and add more value to their lives. I'd greatly appreciate if you send me your feedback directly.
Good Luck!

You might also be interested in reading:

1. **(PART 1)**75 Secrets Revealed on Time Management Skills
http://www.amazon.com/dp/B00K0NVSF8/

2. **(PART 2)** 75 Secrets Revealed on Time Management Skills
http://www.amazon.com/dp/B00KLN2YFU/

3. Time management (2 in 1 Combo offer)
http://www.amazon.com/dp/B00KYQ1SC4/

3. Managing Stress In The Workplace
http://www.amazon.com/dp/B00I0EWO02/

4. 75 Secrets Revealed on Stress, Depression & Anxiety
http://www.amazon.com/dp/B00KYMKHW0/

Image Credits: via freedigitalphotos.net

Designed By nokhoog_buchachon, bplanet, Salvatore Vuono, Stuart Miles, 1shots, arztsamui, jesadaphorn, BrandonSigma, jesadaphorn, imagerymajestic, David Castillo Dominici, graur razvan ionut, jesadaphorn, stockimages, Ambro, and photostock.

OVERVIEW OF MANAGING STRESS IN THE WORKPLACE

http://www.amazon.com/dp/B00I0EWOo
2/

Introduction

Workers worldwide are going through a turbulent phase because of the troubled economy. Words like 'redundancy', 'cut-backs' and 'lay-offs' have become very common. This has resulted in increased levels of stress, anxiety, fear and job insecurities. Workplace stress severely increases during times of economic crisis; hence, it is very essential to learn innovative ways of coping with the building pressure. Mastering the ability to manage workplace stress can make a huge difference between job failure and success. The more you manage your stress levels at the workplace, the more positively you will affect the ones around you.

During these times of economic crisis, it may seem very difficult to cope with the challenges and disputes that arise in the workplace. Workers, managers and employers, irrespective of the industry, are all suffering from aggravated levels of stress; we take stress with us from home and the commute, and more stress awaits us when we get to our jobs. A certain amount of everyday stress is normal; however, excessive distress hampers our productivity, our emotional and physical health, and our working relationships.

Diminishing stress at the workplace is crucial for maintaining your overall health, as it can promote longevity, boost your immune system, and help you in being more productive. Never let your stress get the best of you, because if you do, you not only put yourself at the risk of developing several life-threatening ailments, but you also risk failure.

Stress has a massive impact on your overall wellbeing because it is a natural response activated in the brain. It is therefore essential that you learn ways to keep your stress levels under control at your work-place. Fortunately, there are many effective ways to reduce or eliminate stress at work, and in this book, we will discuss in great detail why stress affects you the way it does, the repercussions of leading a stressful life, and the various ways to combat it success-fully.

Chapter 1

A LATENT GLOBAL EPIDEMIC

"WORKPLACE STRESS"

"It is the usual story. Holding down a job, doing up a home, chairing the Board of Governors at the local comprehensive... it was only in the hospital that I realized how exhausted I was..."

These were the words uttered by Valerie Yates, who had decided to quit her job – sorry, her 'stressful job' – as a marketing director and college board member in Chicago, after she was diagnosed with breast-cancer back in 1997. Fortunately, Mrs. Yates is healthy now, and she gladly admits, "Being away from the office helped me see how stressful and unhealthy it was, how unhealthy – and how much I hated my boss." She adds with a smile of relief, "Life was too short to spend it somewhere like that."

That was in 1997. We are in a whole new era now. However, what Mrs. Yates had suffered back then has now become a part and parcel of our everyday lives. Increasing demands for work efficiency, work output and rising workload have for many employees made the terms 'work' and 'stress' synonymous, which is a sad but hard-hitting truth. If you, my friend, think that you are a victim of stress at your workplace, realize that you are not alone.

Stress at work is now a worldwide phenomenon. Up from a 73% of workers in America in 2012, 84% workers in 2013 had admitted to being stressed by their jobs, according to a 2013 study conducted by Harris Interactive for Everest College, which was published in the November 2013 issue of Forbes magazine. Furthermore, 14% of workers pegged 'low salary' as the leading cause of stress, while 'unreasonable workload' stood a close second, followed by 11% of the workers citing 'commuting' and 'annoying co-workers.' Other stress stimulants included: fear of being fired (4%), lack of opportunity for advancement (6%), poor work-life balance (7%), and the job itself not being the primary career choice (8%). The survey had also revealed that those of the millennial generation –i.e., ages 18 to 29 – tended to express more stress, largely caused by job stability concerns.

In June 2013, the American Psychological Association in New York produced a report that presented the results of their research on increasing stress complaints. According to the report, the data stands as:

Impacts of Stress at Workplace	Average of Victims
People who regularly experience physical symptoms caused by stress	77%
Regularly experience psychological symptoms	73%
Feel thay are living with extreme stress	33%
Feel their stress has increased over past 5 years	48%

That's not all. In addition, the survey also brought to light some of the common symptoms of elevated stress at the workplace, such as anxiety and nervousness (cited by 45% of the workers), lack of energy (45%), irritability and anger (50%), and wanting to cry for relief (35%).

A small glimpse of the large side effects of stress

An old axiom goes like this – "a happy worker is a productive worker." Stress takes its toll not only on individuals, but also on the quantitative and qualitative productivity of firms, companies and workplaces, since these very 'individuals' are their building blocks.

Work-related stress caused workers in Great Britain to lose 10.4 million working days in 2012 and 2013, based on the Labor Force Survey (LFS) conducted by the Office for National Statistics (ONS).

In Canada, data shows that stress-related absenteeism has cost employers losses of $15 to $25 billion in 2012-2013, compared to $3.5 billion in 2003. Roughly 500,000 Canadian workers are absent from the workplace each day due to mental and health-related workplace stress issues. Simultaneously, stress also accounts for 60% of workplace accidents, 19% of absenteeism, 30% of short and long-term disability, and a reduction in turnover of up to 40%.

Chapter 2

AN INTRODUCTION- TO YOUR DAILY 'NECESSARY EVIL'

I am sure you would not disagree that stress is an inevitable part of your everyday 'work' life. You simply cannot ignore it.

However, I suggest you to first view stress as a stimulant. See, stress can motivate a person to be productive and to rise up to face the challenge of tough situations.

Needless to say, we live amidst competing times, and to survive the competition, one always needs to be at the edge. Stress as a positive phenomenon does exactly that – it keeps you on the edge.

However, having said that, we must keep in mind that anything too much or exceeding its limits is negative. For lovers of literature, remember Shakespeare's Macbeth? Too much ambition resulted in an untimely doom. Stress can do exactly that, and often much more.

'Workplace stress is defined as a harmful reaction that people have to endure the pressures and demands placed on them at work.'

The main causes of workplace stress are attributed to work pressure, work-related bullying or violence, and often, lack of managerial support.

These factors cause a 'burnout,' leading to a breakdown, either psychological or physical. You may ask what I mean by 'burnout'. That is exactly what you should do first – ask questions— and talk to yourself regarding your workplace stress patterns. We will follow up this entire study with an elaborate synopsis regarding symptoms, remedies and solutions for stress.

Coming back to burnout, in short, 'stress burnout' is a deep-seated sense of disillusionment and exhaustion with a job or career that used to provide much excitement and motivation. Enthusiasm and passion are gradually stripped away until the drive and will to go on are lost.

I can already see many of you connecting to it. By this time, most of you may now understand that 'stress' is a necessary evil. It is an inevitable part and parcel of your daily lives – a necessary kick to keep you on your toes and allow you to excel. But nevertheless, when it deprives you of your 'life,' it turns evil.

Understanding workplace stress and realizing your limits in enduring it are the most essential steps in your fight against it. So now that you all know what 'stress' is, you are one step closer to controlling it, just like how doctors who can diagnose an illness can proceed down a definite path to treating it.

Chapter 3

TRY AND UNDERSTAND THE PROBLEM

Once you have admitted that you are a victim of stress at the workplace, it becomes easy to combat stress because now you are 'aware' of your position.

Grab a pen and a paper. Try to realize what exactly the reason for your stress is. It may be one cause or more.

Write them down on the paper. You can always use a notebook or an iPhone, android or tablet to type and save the problems; but remember, nothing can replace the art of writing.

When you write, your muscles tend to relax. Your mind focuses on the writing. Now this is very important, because when you are calm, you can recollect, reason and recognize the causes of stress properly.

Yes, writing is a healthy way to keep cool. While writing down the causes of your stress, leave some space beside each one. Whenever you find a possible solution, make an entry on the paper.

Keep the papers with you at all times, especially during office hours, and see that you adhere to the solutions you have written.

There are some common causes of stress. Through a few discussions with some of my friends, I have made a rough idea of what most employees go through. Here on, we will see some prevailing causes of stress and try to work our ways through them for an effective solution.

TOO MANY PROBLEMS? SO ARE THE SOLUTIONS

Workplace stress may not only remain within the boundaries of your office, but also tag along into your personal life. This is one of the psychological hazards of workplace stress.

Another hazard is that it is embedded in the office itself, disguised as work demand, output, meeting the target, deadlines, and so on. In addition to all of these, there are physical hazards too. Violence, work abuse, offensive co-workers, or a bully boss can take a toll on your physical health.

The 'A-class' treatment to your stress problems starts right here – Aware, Analyze, Apply. Being aware is realizing that you are stressed by observing the symptoms, such as headaches, nervousness, excessive worry, increased irritability, and fatigue. You may also realize that you are starting to avoid people and social engagements.

The next step is analysing the causes of stress correctly. Once you know the causes, it is time to apply the appropriate solutions. These three steps form the basis of any kind of planning to combat stress.

Do not get disheartened. For each and every one of these, you can follow a simple "4-As" solution.

1. Avoid
2. Alter
3. Adapt
4. Accept

Remember, every problem has its own unique solution, just like every lock has its key. But these 4 A's are the master key to your solutions to stress in your workplace. There is no reason to go head-on in every matter. You will not become a hero but a victim.

Let's start with the first A – Avoid unnecessary situations.

When you cannot avoid, try to Alter. Change your approach; change your attitude towards the problem and the way to deal with it. Alter your approach to different kinds of people. Do not use the same approach for your co-workers that you use for your boss.

The next two – Adapt and Accept – are on the same plane. Sometimes, you need to accept certain situations and adapt accordingly. Learn to forgive and forget, and try to anticipate by choosing your interpretation of a situation in a more appropriate way.

As we discuss, it will become clearer which of the 4-A's is suitable in which situations.

Chapter 4

UNLOAD THE WORKLOAD

A lot of you must have faced, and are surely still facing, the pressure of an increasing workload, are you not?

Files are piling up, incomplete datasheets are lying around on your desk, the

139

clock is ticking like a time-bomb, and the screen on your laptop is waiting for your next click... what a situation! Can it get any worse than this? Oh yes! Your boss calls and hands over another set of tasks with another deadline.

Relax. The easiest way to set things right is by planning. First of all, what you need to do is TIME MANAGEMENT. Yes, divide your work and set time limits. What aids you in this is planning ahead.

Go to work early and have a glass of water. Relax yourself and see which tasks are pending.

Devote necessary time to each of them as per required, with small five-minute breaks in between. These breaks will help you to relax and revitalize for the next set of tasks.

Utilize your time management skills to shuffle and arrange the data sheets, files and computer programs under common genres. Arrange in separate folders if necessary. Plan and approach, but do not forget to set the proper time limit. This will prevent jumping from one type of work alignment to another.

Believe me, – as one by one, a stack of files or a task is completed, you will breathe a sigh of relief and gain enthusiasm to solve the next one. But do not forget to take small breaks in between.

The next important step is PRIORITIZE. Arrange your tasks according to their importance. Irrespective of whether you like the work for a particular task or not, complete it if it is to be submitted early.

If you are working and you suddenly get a call from your boss asking you to complete a file, do it right then and get it over with. This will keep the boss in good humor and earn you respect.

If you leave the work for later, it will be an added burden and keep distracting you in the back of your mind, and may even interfere with your time management routine. So prioritize your tasks and then take a step forward.

Concentrate on a 'step by step' format

The mind has a limited capacity. If you keep pressuring it and pushing its boundaries, you will surely feel stressed. It is only fair that you concentrate on one goal at a time. Whenever you have a big, elaborate assignment, do not try to complete the whole thing at once. Divide it into parts, and focus on each part with individual details. Follow the 'step by step' format. This will not only allow you to avoid getting stressed, but also make you more productive.

Set a clear objective for yourself

Sometimes, when you do not know where you are going, doubts begin to arise and the tension mounts, leading to a lot of stress. To avoid such pit-falls, it is very important that you set a clear-cut objective before you start working.

Define the objective

This way, you will have an idea of the 'result' you will be working to achieve.

For example, if the assignment involves providing annual data for your workplace, your objective should be to produce a monthly study of the company's profit and loss. Concentrate on each month individually and its turnover. Then provide a chart to compare the monthly and average profits and losses for the whole year. Remember, your mind influences your actions.

So, if you have a planned mindset, your actions will comply with it and give you the desired results.

The next step is something most of us are reluctant to do. Some of you may have guessed it, but it is the time to say 'NO'. See, everyone cannot do everything every time. Do not see this as a drawback. No one is questioning your abilities if you say 'No'. If you already feel burdened with your current work, a heap of additional work will definitely send you off the roof.

Also, accepting a task and not completing it will cause a blot on your performance. This is what you should do – politely give the valid explanation behind your 'No'. Ask your boss to help you out if you do not understand or have any queries regarding the assigned work. Accepting your problem, admitting it and asking for help from your superior will be beneficial to you. Firstly, you will gain respect. Secondly, you can learn from your superior. You may also develop a good work relationship. Judge for yourself, my friend – what will be better for you? Taking an assignment, not completing it and enduring the rage of your boss? Or, saying 'NO' now, then taking on the task when you are capable to handle and complete it, thereby getting goodwill? It is not so tough to choose, is it?

Remember, you can either change the situation or change your course to respond to the situation. 'Focus' is most essential.

1. Focus on what you must do and then what you should do to meet it.
2. Focus on your strengths and how to take care of your drawbacks.

Planning, time management, setting the targets in sequential order according to 'must do' and 'should do', and saying 'no' in the right way will all release you from your stressful position, and that is exactly our goal.

Chapter 5

BE 'AWARE'-

KNOW WHAT YOUR POSITION IS

Stop! Think! Your work is stressing you out, but is it worth it? There are a lot of questions that require your attention, and answering them will help you realize exactly how much pressure you should be feeling in your position at the workplace, and how much extra is burdening you.

Ask yourself, is your commitment towards your work valued? If you are dedicating 8 to 10 hours daily to your work, is your hard work being recognized by higher authorities? If not, ask them for feedback regarding your work, and question them on how you can improve, if it is necessary.

This showcases a positive attitude and seriousness towards your occupation; it will also register you in the 'good' books of your seniors. Secondly, when an assignment or a group task is given to you, clarify the ROLE you are supposed to take on.

Do not, I repeat, do not take on unnecessary burdens by trying to do more than required. Consult your supervisor; ask if you are to be an interpreter, an advisor, or a planner for the assignment. For example, if a group task is given, consider your options. See that you do something substantial. Be the advisor, or be the planner, and work on the layout of the project. If you are comfortable with the layout then make a list, consulting with your group, and gather necessary items and assemble them.

But do not be an architect *and* a planner *and* an interpreter. It will spill the milk.

Thirdly, as I mentioned, see that you are doing something substantial. Ask yourself – is my job or my work meaningful? If yes, then how is it meaningful? If no, then how can I make it better? Often times, we feel depressed when after hours of hard work, we do not get the desired results. Does that mean that you, I, we are all failures? Not at all. What it does mean is that our work may not have been recognized. Approach your supervisor or superior and calmly present your work. Make them take notice of your effort. At least you will be glad that you tried your best. Feeling good about yourself will help reduce the stress.

Next, ask one important question – what are your POSSIBILITIES for DEVELOPMENT? Think of your development as an individual and as an employee, and how your work environment can accelerate your growth. If you find that your work environment is not suitable, consider altering it. How can you better yourself in this environment? Should you change your workplace? Consider your options carefully. Remember, progress can never be stagnant; it is progressive.

The most important question to be considered is regarding DISCRIMINATION. Discrimination based on color, status and sex is equivalent to criminal assault. If you are a victim, do not be scared or depressed. Remember, you can approach the judicial doors; it is your right. Know your company's policies and procedures properly. Keep a hard copy in your bag. Whenever you feel harassment owing to discrimination, contact your superior and highlight the policies on discrimination. If things do not improve, document all conversations with your co-workers and boss, be it verbal or via email or messages. You can consult your HR or a jury, if needed, with substantial evidence.

The Civil Rights Act makes it illegal to discriminate on grounds of class, race, gender, color, religion or national origin. Hence, know your 'position'. As a responsible citizen, you deserve equal treatment, so know your rights. There is nothing shameful about asking for what is rightfully yours.

OVERVIEW OF Time Management Book

(2 in 1 Combo of-fer)

http://www.amazon.com/dp/B00KYQ1SC4
/

Chapter 1

5 Habits of Extremely Effective Mediocre People

I am a jack of all trades and master of none. I have never done anything that grabs eyeballs, like writing a bestseller, winning a national level championship, owning a million-dollar company, funding cancer research or visiting outer space. I have had my fair share of failures and successes, but I have never accomplished any of the targets that I had initially fixed.

I fail at most of my endeavors, make bad investments, withdraw into a shell and drown in hopelessness. I have tried my hand at writing before but ended up quitting halfway, and learnt to cook various cuisines but started disliking them. I paint, but do not be mistaken, my creations are hardly masterpieces.

Success is to be measured not so much by the position that one has reached in life as by the obstacles which he has overcome. - **Booker T. Washington**

I also have insomnia, which means I spend my nights half-awake, rolling in bed, watching the clock tick, and even worse, my days are filled with drowsiness. I am sleep deprived, overworked and exhausted. It gets so bad that sometimes if I am lucky enough to catch a flick in the theater, I fall asleep, even if the movie is jaw dropping and a blockbuster hit.

I keep changing my diet, I read a lot of new information, set goals and get myself completely psyched up and keep telling myself that I can do it. But after a few weeks, I fizzle, seemingly unable to stick to the promises I make. I have many other issues that quick fix approaches can't fix, and writing is my gateway to freedom and exhilaration. Overall, everything I have done has been identified by its mediocrity, and most people associate my success with luck.

That being said, it's very obvious that all of us cannot be great illusionists. We can't all be Mozarts, Beethovens or Picassos. Luck seldom favors us, and everyone is not born with a silver spoon. However, we do want to make good money, enjoy life's luxuries, nurture a healthy family and be happy. You have to aim for the stars but keep your foot firmly on the ground. Aiming for ornateness is always a recipe for disaster. So don't sweat it; if you are a perfectly average person like me and want to make the most of everything, then take a look at my recommendations.

There is no real excellence in all this world that can be separated from right living- **David Star Jordan**

• **Focusing on getting better, rather than being good:**

Nobody is perfect from the get-go. We make progress over time, after countless trials and tribulations. Focusing precisely on getting better is a very lucrative habit, because people who exercise it experience less stress and anxiety, even in the face of terrible turbulence. It enables a person to handle negative emotions, pessimistic thoughts, negative feedback and bad criticism in a much more positive way.

It is very crucial to have interest and enjoy what you are doing, in order to master your skills and accomplish success. The ones who concentrate on incurring better outputs are much more capable of handling failures and overcoming obstacles. The ones who have the 'get better' mindset are always the peak performers.

Many of us believe that our aptitudes and abilities are fixed, and that they cannot improve or deteriorate with time and effort. As a result of this belief, we only focus on those goals and targets that are only about proving how good we are, rather than acquiring, developing and mastering new skills.

Luckily, decades of behavioral research has profoundly proved that 'belief in only fixed ability' is absolutely wrong. Abilities and skills of all types and kinds are deeply tensile. People whose ambition is all about getting better in their respective fields bravely take difficulty in their stride and appreciate the journey as much as the destination.

- **Learning to say 'No':**

*The difference between successful people and very successful people is that very successful people say 'no' to almost everything- **Warren Buffet***

Saying 'No', makes you look impolite, selfish, aloof, rude, and even anti-social. However, 'No' is the only word that takes us ahead of others and maintains our sanity. Initially, I had a lot of difficulty saying 'No', especially to my family and friends. I always tried to seem modest and polite, at my expense. For example, whenever I received any requests for assistance, I would always attend to them, even though I had other essential chores to complete.
Sometimes these requests would stretch way beyond 4-5 hours or even days. Ultimately, I would end up hampering my work and disrupting my schedule. I would forfeit my holidays, sleep less, clog my schedule and make up for all the pending work.

However, no matter how hard I tried, I could never make up for all the lost time and opportunities. This was also a very common phenomenon in my professional life, and I suffered a lot for it. It hindered my performance and made me frantic.

Gradually, I understood that my inability to say 'No' was taking a toll on my work and life. I realized that this awful habit was devastating me. My own time and energy were spent on solving other's issues, rather than my own. It was very frustrating since I was asking for it. Eventually, I realized, in order to get out of this mortifying situation, I had to learn to say 'No' and exercise it to the best of my abilities.

- **Not Tempting Fate:**

Success is not just about being at the right place at the right time. This is simply a component of success; there's also the significant involvement of hard work, persistence and perseverance. Restraining yourself from executing an idea by waiting for the perfect time, situation, place and position is a folly.

Brainstorming is significant, but, like Robin Sharma rightly said, "ideation without execution is an illusion." Most superbly successful people got to where they are by launching themselves immediately, even if the timing or circumstance wasn't perfect.

Time waits for nobody; we have to realize a simple logic that 'if today the time isn't perfect, then it never will be.'

We have to understand that no matter how strong-willed we are, there will be times when our self-will or command will be low, situations or circumstances will be rough and places will be unsuitable or hostile. Hence, we have to understand the significance of resisting temptation and not putting ourselves in harm's way. We have to stop leaning, depending or inclining towards fate. It's a tough one, but practice makes perfect.

• **Avoiding Multitasking:**

Multitasking is a recipe for disaster. It's a common myth that all successful people multitask. Maybe some great people do, but most of us do not; consequently, it's much better to single-task. Even now, you might be reading this post while doing your laundry, watching TV, cooking, gardening, bathing, and so on. Today, we are all hell bent on multitasking, since we are hooked into our iPods, iPads and iPhones, not to mention the TV, computers, and consoles. I always have too much to do and too little time.

Your perception is that you are trying to save as much time as possible by doing multiple things at once. The real truth is, you are actually wasting a lot of time, because you are solely focusing on none. Of course, your meal will be ready, the garden will be prepped, and laundry will be done, but you will hardly remember anything that you have watched on TV or read in this post, and the quality of the rest of the items will suffer as well.

You might assume that you are good at multitasking, but multitasking itself is a futile engagement. Our brains aren't equipped to handle multitasking, but it might fool us into believing that we can. Recent studies have proved that the brain is not built for multitasking. While attempting multitasking, the brain shuts down one task to accomplish the other, which causes a delay in brain operation, and everything takes longer than usual. When the tasks are dissimilar and require some degree of attention, multitasking falls apart.

It makes us less productive, deteriorates our work output and makes our lives haphazard. Once you stop multitasking and start single tasking, you will start climbing up the ladder much faster than before.

So, instead of reading this post and doing tons of other things, try something different. Practice aerobics, do yoga, go for a walk, swim, run or simply listen to some soothing music. Give your brain a break. The rest can wait.

- **Embracing Incessant Failures:**

No matter how hard you try to avoid it, failure will occur. Successful people understand the reality and inevitability of failure and its contribution in imparting success. Hence, embracing it is a much easier option than escaping it. You cannot escape it, as it will follow you everywhere. Just do not commit the same mistakes again; make new ones and learn from the old ones.

It took some time, effort and errors for this realization to dawn on me. I used to be very skeptical about my endeavors because of the prospect of failure. I have made numerous mistakes in my business, and I am embarrassed to recount most of them.

There are examples of people who have rarely failed, like Mark Zuckerberg, Bill Gates, and Larry Page, but those are great visionaries who have altered the face of mankind. In comparison, most of us are pretty mediocre; we strive for greatness but rarely achieve it. However, we make many mistakes along the way.

So, in order to achieve what we desire, we will have to learn to embrace all our mistakes, study them and move ahead. The cliche, "Keep going until you hit the finish line" sounds great, but for all the mediocre, average entrepreneurs, "Keep failing until you no longer fail" is better suited.

Chapter 2

5 Tips to Do a Monthly Review

Each day has been mapped out for us. From a very young age, everything has been decided for us. Which school we go to, the classes we attend. Everything is planned. However, we find a huge change once we move on to college and work. Everything is now our decision. Our plans fly out the window, and every day is unplanned and chaotic.

This is why we have time management programs that help us organize our lives. Time management skills are something that one does not have to be born with; they can be developed in a person. Without a proper work schedule, you can be faced with many problems. You may find yourselves buried under piles of work and obligations.

Before you learn the ways to review your work, you need to know how to classify your month to make it easy for you. First, separate your month as week 1, week 2 and maintain a notebook for that. For each week of the month, plan your workdays. This will help you lessen your burden each month.

Planning for each week will require your time, so make sure you have allotted an hour or so for this, preferably on the weekend. Sit down and plan your upcoming days and classify your work according to your convenience. This weekly breakdown will also help you review the work of the previous week, if you feel that is necessary. Make sure you write the events on a calendar or your phone to remind you of your schedule.

Make a note of whatever you need to do. If you need to do your laundry or call your mother, make sure you have written it down somewhere. Remember, your brain is like a computer; the more it tries to remember, the more energy it will use. After you have a grasp of managing your time, you can move on to reviewing your work.

Here are 5 tips to help you review your ability to manage time on a monthly basis:

• **Have a particular day to "check in":** Every month, make sure you set a day to review your work. You may be surprised by what you find when you review your accomplishments! Examining your monthly accomplishments and failures will show you where you stand. Are you working according to your values? Have you accomplished the goals you set out to do? If you were unable to do so, why? Critically analyzing what you could have done better will help you tremendously.

• **What you failed to accomplish:** Make sure you have a fixed goal that you

162

would like to achieve every month. You may have had a project that was due by the end of the month. Analyze why you were unable to finish the project and whether you should pursue it. Do not let unfinished projects let you down; if you are unable to finish it within the stipulated time, leave it.

• **List things you want to change:** You may want to change a few "negative" traits in you, be it work or personal. Change some strategies to get better offers from your clients. Make a list of the things you would like to change and implement the changes. Your change may be more personal than work related; this is not wrong. Do not feel personal changes is secondary. Write it down, as it might affect your work in other ways. For example, it may boost your confidence, which in turn will help you talk to clients and boost the company's image. Make sure your goals are properly documented and remind yourself of the changes you want to make.

• **Take note of your goals:** Break down your goals and put categorize them into daily goals and weekly goals. Make sure you jot down deadlines to help you remember. Do not be shy to write down your personal goals too. If you want to lose some weight, or take a course, jot them down in your planner. It helps you keep track of your days and prevents time clashes. Remember time management is not only working for lesser amounts of time, but also the smart management of time.

• **Reminders:** Make sure you set many reminders to keep track of your meetings and other activities. Keep reminders on phones, planners and even your mirrors if that helps! This will keep you on your toes. If you feel this will not help you, ask your co-worker to remind you of a certain task. Nothing makes you work like encouragement, regardless of whom it is from.

Make sure you have no distractions when you review yourself. Go to a quiet place like your room or office and analyze your month. If you cannot find a quiet place, book a hotel room or go to a friend's house.

These weekly and monthly reviews are very important to help keep track of your goals. Take small steps every day to achieve your goals. Without reviewing yourself, you cannot aim to achieve your goals within the set time period.

If you want your plans to be carried out successfully, make sure you follow these monthly reviews regularly. Without a proper structure for your week or month, you can become stressed. Your work becomes sloppy, and you tend to be in a bad mood. To avoid such disasters, review your work frequently. These reviews will help you know where you stand.

Your monthly reviews are also good for another purpose – planning the goals for your next month. It also helps you by giving an idea of what activities you can look forward to. Once you review your month and analyze your outcome, it will lead to two things: it will make you a better planner and keep your activities on par with your schedule, and it will make you disciplined.

Remember, these monthly reviews will probably take up only an hour or two of your time. Reviewing your work is as important as planning it, especially when you want to manage your time. Analyze your failures and achievements for that month. This will give you an idea of your strengths and weaknesses. You will now know how you can better yourself and do this in a shorter span of time. Practice makes you perfect; reviewing your work makes you even more so.

Chapter 3

5 Tips to Do a Task, even if You Are Not in the Mood to Do It

Motivation doesn't come easy. Often, we find ourselves grunting and complaining when we are trying to finish a boring task. Sometimes, it isn't just boredom that prevents us from doing the job; it's the task itself. This is understandable, as boring and arduous tasks do not really motivate us. We procrastinate, give excuses and end up do-ing anything but the job.

This cycle can tamper with work enormous-ly, and that is dangerous – both for our work and motivation levels.
So, what do you do when you have piles of work, but you are not in the mood to finish it?

• **Do it NOW:**

The first sign of procrastination is when you come up with crafty excuses to postpone your work. When you find that your excuses are getting more and more creative, you should stop there. Put a full-stop to these thoughts.

When you stop feeding this never-ending pot of excuses, you will find yourself doing your job. What's more is that you might even be interested in it now. It is safe to say that everyone has some task that they dis-like doing. The only way around it is to start doing the task and finish it off before you can over-think it.

Psychologists have proved that when you reach a goal, your brain releases pleasure chemicals. Thus, postponing your job doesn't help you at the least.

When you do the work without delay, you not only get to cross something off the list, but also get to feel victorious. You conquered yourself and your moods.

So, next time you feel lazy or bored, finishing work will not pose to be such a problem.

- **Time-box it:**

Time-boxing is an especially useful method that helps you complete a task. It encompasses all the essential items through which you can organize yourself.

A simple example can illustrate the technique of time-boxing: Say you have a project to complete within a deadline. Because you have a fixed time limit, you spend your time wisely and in the best way possible.

One reason why this technique is very effective is due to the reward factor. Before you set out on your task, choose a reward you can give yourself at the end of the set time frame. This could be a movie or half an hour of your favorite TV-show.

Time-boxing is a highly individualistic technique. You get to decide the reward at the end of the time you put in. Also, you decide how long to work for.

Sometimes, your time-boxes can be split on an hourly basis. At the end of each hour, make sure you have a small reward. The work-reward system is directly proportionate; the more time you work, the bigger the reward you get. Many management gurus ask beginners to start with a thirty-minute time frame. You can gradually move on and work for one or two hours at a time.

One sure benefit that can be gained from following this technique is that you gradually become interested in doing the task. Once you actually get onto finishing the task, you get involved in it. Therefore, you put in extra time into finishing the task. And an additional bonus is that your reward will be waiting for you at the end. You can go and claim it whenever you are done.

The psychology of this technique is that you tend to work more when you have short-term goals and rewards, rather than long-term ones.

•   **Time-Schedule your work:**

Time-scheduling is a fairly simple technique. By following this technique, you estimate the maximum time that you will devote to a task. Setting the time frame could be a problem, as each task is different. Follow a rather scientific approach and evaluate the task. If the task at hand is extremely distasteful, then add an extra half hour to the estimated time of completion.

If you've allotted two hours to complete a presentation, and you aren't in the mood to finish it, then add an extra half hour. This way, you methodically list out the estimated time limits and ultimately, you follow this time table. Additionally, by taking care of discrepancies, you ensure that the little breaks are accounted for.

- **Good habits are hard to break:**

When you despise a task with passion, make sure you do it every day. When you repeat the task over and over again, you will get accustomed to it. As a result of the familiarity, the task will not bore you. You can complete it before you even know it.

Most bloggers and writers follow this practice. Even though laziness strikes them often, they force themselves to finish their write-up. This helps a lot. Since you know you will have to complete it, you ultimately try finishing it more quickly. This is just so you can move onto a more pleasant task.

• Accountability partners can make it work:

Successful CEOs say you can finish a task by getting an Accountability Partner. The concept of an Accountability Partner is simple. You get a person you can trust to ensure that you are working according to schedule. When you promise yourself something, you are more likely to break it. However, when you promise your friend or a relative, you will be motivated to keep the promise, as you are accountable to them as well.

This way, you have someone else to answer to. And when you don't answer just to yourself, but others as well, you automatically become more responsible.

Bad moods are persistent, and they pull you down. They can come in different ways – anger and boredom, to name a few. The end result is that it deeply affects your work. When you aren't motivated to finish a task, your reputation may be affected. You lose opportunities, and sadly, your learning quotient also goes down.

Whatever the cause might be, you don't feel like working. So, you postpone. When that happens, it becomes a dangerous habit. Procrastination makes a person lazy and de-motivated.

When you take simple steps to fight it, you learn the value of time.

Chapter 4

5 Tips to Find One Day a Week to Complete All Your Pending Work

Time and tide wait for none. The most valuable thing money cannot buy is time. With so much work pressure these days, you might find it very difficult to manage time. You might have a lot of pending work at the end of the week.

If you don't complete the pending work then and there, it might start accumulating. So one option is to work smartly and allocate a separate day to finish the pending work. You don't have to work for hours to get everything done, but you do have to use time efficiently to get it all done in a short span of time. This is where time management comes in. To change the way things are happening, first we have to change ourselves.

If you work efficiently each day, you can get more work done. Find one day a week to complete all the work pending for that week. It is better to complete all the important tasks first.

Here are a few strategies you can use to manage your time efficiently.

- **Plan your week ahead**

The first step in managing your time efficiently is planning your week ahead. If you manage all the days of a week properly, then you will be able to find a day to finish all your pending work. Write down all the important events that are coming up and prioritize them. Assign time slots to each task based on its importance. Planning gives you a feeling that you have good control over your life, thereby boosting your self-esteem.

• Prioritize your work

There is a rule called the 80/20 rule. According to this rule, 80% of the value of one's day is based on 20% of the work he does.

So if you start focusing more on that 20%, you will be more productive, as you will do the more important work first.

If you cannot complete the task, move it to the pending list; or if it is very important, move it to the next day. You can do all the jobs on the pending list after all the important tasks are completed. Don't be shy to ask for help. Nobody can do everything by themselves.

You have to be flexible and change your strategies based on the circumstances. And learn to politely say 'No' without being blunt. Justify why you cannot help them; for example, show them your schedule and make them understand. So if you plan your week well, you will definitely find a day in the week to finish your pending work.

- **Plan your day ahead**

Planning your day is important in executing all the tasks as planned. If you complete as many tasks as possible, you can prevent work from being added to the 'pending' list.

Finish the important work first. Allot time for everything that's important. Plan the day either the previous night or during the first 30 minutes of the day. Have a checklist of the tasks, and keep crossing them out as you finish them. Try not to keep any pending work. If you are not able to complete a task, carry it over to the next day. Don't let it disturb what you have planned for the rest of the day.

Start each task as early as possible. Some tasks may take more time than expected. Add buffer time between tasks. This will let you finish each task properly, and if you need to take care of other emergencies, buffer time will be of great help. You can use Google Calendar to mark all the events, and adding an organizer will be useful to organize the to-do lists.

At the same time, don't plan too much for the day. Overloading yourself will only cause you to break down. When at work, keep your phones and laptops away from you. Don't check your emails or Facebook notifications too often. They will consume your time without your knowledge. Instead, allot time for social networking or to check your emails, and stick to it. Turn off the noise that alerts you when you get an email. Do not try to multi-task, as it will only lower your efficiency. You might be side-tracked from doing what's more important. Do one thing at a time.

Use online timers like Egg Timer to keep track of your time. Finish the unpleasant tasks as soon as possible. This way, you will not have to postpone it for the next day.

• **Balance each day**

Don't overload yourself with too many tasks. Distribute them over the week. If you overload yourself, you will get tired, bring-ing down your efficiency. Balance each day and do as much as you can, but at the same time, be sure to spend time with your friends and family. You don't have to sacri-fice your work time to do that. It just needs to be balanced. If you spend a little time with your family every day, you will not have to specially allocate a whole day for them.

When at work, do not spend time on any other activity, so that you will not have pending work to carry over. Plus, when your work starts piling up as pending, you will feel stressed out. It will take away the time you plan to spend with your friends and family. It will also make you lose your self-confidence and feel de-motivated.

So when you allot particular time for an activity, never let anything else interrupt you. And never leave any job incomplete. It takes more time to finish a job that's left incomplete. You will miss the flow. When you complete the job, take short breaks. This will motivate you and prevent you from having too much pending work. You could go for a walk outside or have a cup of coffee. Set reminders to take breaks.

A few of us might prefer working at a stretch before taking breaks. Others may prefer taking shorter breaks more often. If you start conversing with your colleague, make sure you don't lose track of time. Don't take long breaks. When you balance each day, you can complete most of your work. You can use a day of the week just to complete the pending work.

• **Adjust your work pattern**

Habits play an important role in time management, especially for those of you who work from home. Taking rest for a whole day and working for the whole of the next might not give you great results. Develop habits that suit your work lifestyle. Habits should make you more efficient and productive.

Going to bed early, waking up early, eating healthy food and exercising regularly can make you feel energetic and more efficient. Never sleep less. Always sleep for a minimum of 7 hours a day, or else you can develop health problems.

There are several strategies for time management, and these are just some of them. Time management strategies have to be customized depending on the work and time each person has. But without proper time management, life will be chaotic.

By following these basic strategies, you can manage time effectively. You will see your productivity increase. It will be easier to balance your life. Try it out, and good luck!

OVERVIEW OF

75 Secrets Revealed on Stres, Depression & Anxiety Book

http://www.amazon.com/dp/B00KYMKHWo/

Chapter 1

5 Tips To Use Self-hypnosis To Reduce Stress

Stress is our very own monster of the 21st century. We, who practically survive on Red Bull and coffee, whose existences revolve around the laptop screen, who always seem to bite more than we can chew, are its beloved victims.

It eats us up from within, like a bloodthirsty parasite. It causes us intense bodily and mental discomfort, and if not handled properly, can damage us for life! Out of the many clinically approved stress-fighting strategies, self-hypnotism is one of the foremost methods that are recommended by counselors around the globe.

It isn't a new way to battle stress, but rather, an age-old therapeutic technique that was pioneered by James Braid in 1841, when he cured his own rheumatism by hypnotizing himself. Since then, it has been taken up by well-known figures and has led to innovations. But the core principles remain the same.

Here are 5 simple tips to use self-hypnosis to reduce stress:

• **Relaxation** – There's nothing like relaxation to soothe a weary mind. Put on loose, comfortable clothes and sit down somewhere you know you won't be disturbed.

Close your eyes. Take deep breaths. Settle down in a comfortable position, but don't lie down. Spend some quality time with yourself. Talk to yourself.

Getting to that fully relaxed state that renders successful self-hypnotism is half the job done, and also the hardest step to accomplish.

Self-hypnotism is like a great 'voyage of discovery' that leads you to know yourself better. So be conversant with yourself. Stress fragments your 'self' and estranges each piece from the other. Start a process of internal integration via relaxation.

• **Managing Emotions** – The first step is to acknowledge the powerful influence that emotions have over us. But there are various kinds of such emotional forces.

The positive, proactive kinds push you toward your goals and help you fly high, whereas the negative, retroactive ones hold you back, generate self-doubt and almost always incapacitate you in the face of stress. You have to learn to pick the emotions you think will be an advantage to you and discard the ones you feel bring you down.

Don't forget that self-hypnosis is a powerful tool and can seriously disrupt your life if not used appropriately. It is mandatory that you focus on knowing yourself before you start the process so that you know what to endorse and what to push back when you enter the realm of self-hypnosis.

• **Goals** – You should have clear and concrete goals before you hypnotize yourself. Search inside yourself, find out what they are, and give them a discernible form. Gather up your sticky notes, make lists, and jot down all the things you want to improve in your life. Keep them close and work to learn them by heart, so that when you sit down to engage in self-hypnotism, you have them near at hand.

For instance, if you want yourself to worry less, write that down in large letters and place it somewhere you can see from your designated spot. When you start the process, focus your thoughts on those goals. Initially, go with anyone one goal, but later, as you grow more and more adept at this, you can pick up more than one goal and concentrate on them all.

• **Creative Visualizations** – Self-hypnosis is incomplete without creative visualizations. Keep your mind open, but don't let it scatter in all directions.

Focus on single images and try to live in them, feel them. Establish a sequence in these images. Picture yourself stepping from one set of events into another in a definite sequence. Your actions within these imaginings should be determined and planned. Try to avoid ambiguity and diffuseness, as you're trying to convince yourself of something. It won't help if that thing is poorly defined.

Also, visualizing isn't a passive process. You need to be a part of it as well, for it to be fully effective. You have to activate your senses within that sphere of creative imagination, so you fully feel, both physically and mentally, what you're imagining. For instance, if you visualize that you're flying, you should also be able to feel the wind in your hair, smell the aroma of the sky and feel the glare of the sun in your eyes.

• **Positivity** – The way you phrase your statements is significant as well. Think along the lines of "I am such-and-such" or "I can do such-and-such" rather than "I don't want to be such-and-such." Believe me, it helps. A little positivity can do wonders to your life.

With positive statements, you find it easier to believe and accept that you actually have the qualities you long to possess, and self-hypnotism's goal is more easily achieved. You slowly build up confidence in yourself and boost your strength to put up with stress, while negativity only leads to low self-esteem and self-pity, which gradually cripple you. Think and be positive, and notice the change this brings in the way you see the world.

Self-hypnotic techniques are discussed in great detail in many health magazines and websites, but by following the techniques above, you can make them extra-effective and more helpful in relieving stress. Our monsters are our own to defeat. We can be helped only to the extent of being advised or suggested what to do. At the end of the day, it's up to us whether we slay the stress-monster or keep feeding it with our weakness and negativity. I'd choose the former any day, but what about you? Will you step up? Will you make a change?

Start today, then, as life is just too short to be spent under stress.

Chapter 2

5 Ways How Cognitive Behavioral Therapy Can Reduce Depression

Cognitive behavioral therapy (CBT) is a psychotherapeutic treatment that is used to reduce depression. CBT is a form of talking therapy.

It is one of the most effective treatments for problems involving depression or anxiety. This therapy can be used to treat both severe and moderate depression. It works better than anti-depressants.

However, for severe depression, one has to take anti-depressants along with the treatment. CBT is also used to treat various mental disorders, like phobias, anxiety, depression, bulimia, stress, post-traumatic stress disorder, bipolar disorder, psychosis, obsessive compulsive disorder, eating disorders and addiction.

It is also used to treat people with long-term health problems, like arthritis and irritable bowel syndrome. CBT helps to change your thinking ('cognitive') and what you do ('behavior'). It cannot improve your physical health, but it can help you to better cope with these problems.

Unlike psychotherapy, which focuses on your past, this therapy deals with your current problems. CBT helps patients understand the thoughts and feelings influencing their behaviors. It is based on the principle that our thoughts and feelings play a fundamental role in our behavior.

Here are 5 ways how CBT can reduce depression:

- **Thought records**

This technique is used to justify one's thoughts. Consider a student who gets bad grades, and his teacher gives feedback that he's disappointed. The student might assume that his teacher thinks he's a bad student. Then he could analyze that thought by collecting the points supporting and opposing that.

A point opposing the thought may be that the teacher still gives the student some responsibilities.

The next step is to create balanced thoughts. "The teacher gave me negative feedback to correct me out of his genuine concern. And it is absolutely normal to make mistakes. Mistakes teach us lessons. I can impress my teacher if I take his feedback and rectify my mistakes."
Thought records help change the thoughts. Behavioral experiments help change the beliefs at a gut level.

189

- **Behavioral experiments**

This is one of the most effective techniques in CBT. Behavioral experimenting is a technique designed to test the validity of thoughts.

For example, you might do a behavioral experiment to test the thought "If I criticize myself after overeating, I will stop overeating" versus "If I talk to myself kindly and motivate myself after overeating, I will stop overeating".
To test these thoughts, you would have to try each approach on different occasions and note the subsequent results. This will give you a clear idea of whether self-criticism or self-kindness helps.

- **Including fun activities**

This is an effective technique that is particularly very helpful for those suffering from depression. Schedule one enjoyable activity for a day. The activity should be something that you enjoy doing that's not unhealthy and that you normally don't do.

It can be anything like listening to your favorite song or talking to your long-lost friend. It should take less than 10 minutes of your time. Or you can do one in the morning, one in the afternoon and another in the evening.

These activities will make you feel good and boost your positivity.

• Overcoming the fear by exposure

For this CBT technique, you list all those activities you would avoid. A person whose eating habits are unhealthy will create a list based on what he should avoid more. Junk food would have higher 'to avoid' rating than dairy.

A person who has an inferiority complex will make his own list, with a date topping the list and a movie with his colleagues at the bottom. After listing the things to avoid, rate them on a scale of 0-10 based on how distressed you'll feel if you had to do it.

For example, a date= 10, social event= 5 and asking a woman for directions= 2. Arrange them in descending order based on the rating you've given them. Try writing down more situations for every distress rating. This way, you will not have big jumps.

Start with the activities that have the lowest distress rating and move slowly to the top of the list. The idea is to try each item on the list several times until you feel more comfortable and less distressed about it. You should be less distressed by at least half of how you felt about in the beginning.

That is, if the distress rating at the beginning was 2, now it should be reduced to 1 before you move up the list.

•   **Recalling the past**

This is another CBT technique, and it involves recalling a recent event that had a huge impact on your emotions.

Let's consider a person receiving negative feedback from his supervisor.

In this technique, the person will visually and emotionally recall the memory of getting the negative feedback. He'd recollect how his senses felt. That is, the tone of the supervisor's voice, how the surrounding looked and the emotions he went through.

This therapy is preferred by both treatment professionals and those suffering from mental disorders. It has a reputation of being effective in helping patients with maladaptive behaviors. As CBT is a short-term treatment, it is more affordable; however, it is a difficult process, especially for patients who cannot introspect themselves.

So it may not be suitable for those with more complex mental health needs and those with learning difficulties.

But ultimately, self-discovery and insights are the essential components of the treatment process. The patient starts learning and practicing new skills to be used in real-life situations.

The main highlight of this therapy is that it focuses on highly specific goals. It is more suitable for patients who are comfortable with introspection.

For the treatment to be a success, the individual must be ready and cooperative. He must be willing to spend time and effort in analyzing his thoughts and feelings. This self-analysis may be difficult, but it is a great way to learn how emotions influence outward behavior.

Another advantage is that it is a great option for those seeking a short-term treatment option. It does not necessarily involve medication.

It helps the client develop coping skills that will be useful not only for the present, but also for the future.

Chapter 3

5 Ways How Bibliotherapy Can Beat Depression

Books can be the best companions.

All one has to do is embrace the wonders of reading. It can provide great companionship to all. Depression is a serious issue that can affect anyone – children, teenagers, adults and the elderly. Certain books are designed to help depressed individuals to cope with their problems. Bibliotherapy is not restricted to reading or books. It also includes related fields.

•   It's   best   to   avoid   anti-depressants (until and unless your therapist recommends them)

Anti-depressants or drugs are not always apt solutions. Intake of drugs can cause a lot of side effects. It is also believed that the placebo effect plays a large role. If that is the case, drugs only cause a temporary clearing of the haze of depression.

Books can provide an apt distraction. They are a better option compared to anti-depressants. Self-help books explain the symptoms and causes of depression, and also provide solutions. These books are written by experts on matters of the mind and are recommended by psychologists and psychiatrists.

<u>It is not advisable to initiate one's own treatment. It is better to seek professional opinion.</u>

Books like the Bible or the Bhagavad Gita are also helpful. To the aged, spiritual and religious books may offer solace. The philo-sophical content provides a way out of depression.

- **Fiction as a fun and viable solution**

Bibliotherapy does not have to consist of non-fiction books. Fiction is also a great choice. Books are the pathway to a new realm. They take the readers on a grand adventure.

Books are often considered as a means of escape. This is partially true, but there is a whole other side to it that is not understood. Poetry, drama and prose often have stories and plots that appeal to those suffering from depression.

All stories contain a message – obvious or otherwise. For people plagued by depression, the message matters more than anything else. They see characters undergoing difficulties and finding means to emerge victorious in their pursuits. They imagine themselves as the protagonists and feel better knowing that they have company.

The course of the book helps them take a step forward in their own lives, and a happy ending motivates them to seek their own.

- **Companions come in all forms**

There are support groups for nearly all sorts of disorders, and as such, there are reading groups for depressed people. Members get together and share their anxiety with each other. Then they read together and embark on a journey.

Bibliotherapy draws the readers into relatable and empathetic subjects, which help them cope with their depression. It also inspires readers and encourages them to read. A discussion follows as to why the book was chosen and how it has benefitted the reader.

The elderly face the issue of abandonment and subsequent depression. They take comfort in knowing that they are not the only ones affected. Companionship is an instrument for healing. Books do the rest.

Reading groups are also a social gathering. When people meet fellow human beings and spend time together, they let go of their problems for a while and enjoy the communal session.

• **Stories and pictures**

When faced with emotional or physical abuse, children often withdraw from reality and keep to themselves. They fear abrupt changes and choose to rebel against the causes for change. Bibliotherapy is not just about reading; it can also involve drawing.

Therefore, especially for children who suffer from depression, any scene from a book that appeals to them can be taken and expressed in the form of images. Expressing oneself is an important component in beating depression. Children also find an outlet in the form of narrating stories. They are encouraged to base the characters on their lives and spin a tale.

There are three stages of bibliotherapy:

- **Identification** – readers associate themselves with the characters in the literary work.
- **Catharsis** – readers share emotions and ideas of the characters.
- **Insight** – readers relate to the characters and deal with their problems.

Teachers are almost always the first ones to notice disorders in children. It is the teachers' responsibility to choose ideal books for the children. They help the student undergo the three stages.

- **Dear diary**

Teenagers are probably the most misunderstood segment of society. They are at an age when they can neither be treated as children nor as adults. They undergo changes in their body and emotions. They fancy themselves to be in love and then face disappointment. Many teenagers witness the divorce of their parents. It is at this age that they are labeled into categories – geeks, jocks, prom queens or wallflowers. They are also pressured into making career decisions. It can be one or a combination of a few of these things that cause them to spiral into depression.

The current generation scorns books and are averse to reading. Writing is also a choice of expression. Teenagers can confess their emotions to their faithful diary, which guards their secrets. They let their feelings out and often feel less burdened. They also write poetry or song lyrics, which express their deep emotions. Sometime later, when they read their own writings, they remember what they had gone through and are reminded never to repeat the same mistakes.

Depression is not a disease. It is a disorder and not one to be taken lightly. Various reasons cause people of different age groups to plunge into a state of nearly eternal misery. Abuse, neglect, separation and abandonment are few of the reasons why people sink into depression. Bibliotherapy is a universal solution. There are books to cater to the requirements of everyone. There are various genres of fiction and non-fiction books. With the right guidance and book, depression can easily be combated.

Other forms of bibliotherapy, like sketching, story-telling and jotting down your thoughts, are equally effective. A vent, an outpouring, a means of expression is all that is required to shake off the misery.

Books, including diaries, are one of the most trustworthy companions. They safeguard one's secrets and provide a distraction from the strenuous world.

Befriend a book, share it with your friends and forget depression.

Chapter 4

5 Nutritional Deficiencies That Can Cause Depression

Approximately 40% of adults in the U.S. suffer from depression. Several leading researchers have concluded that depression is not just caused by overwhelming sadness. Often, this psychological condition is related closely to our food choices.

One day, we are happy, and a month later, we are exhausted and irritated. Many people often complain that they do not know why they are depressed. Doctors have pointed out that deficiencies of certain nutrients can trigger depression.

Our body is made in such a way that we require an intricate balance of essential nutrients. When we do not have sufficient nutrients in our body, we are prone to chemical and hormonal imbalances. These imbalances trigger and accelerate depression and anxiety.

Here are five nutrients whose deficiency can cause depression:

- **Vitamin B-12 deficiency:**

When a person goes for a counseling session with a psychologist for the first time, they will be asked to go for a full-body checkup. In the prescription itself, the doctor asks the patient to take a specific test to measure the levels of vitamin B-12 in our body.

Our body produces certain chemicals that are vital for the stability of our moods. Sometimes, when we fall short of a certain nutrient, our entire system can go haywire. A nutritional deficiency that is linked to depression is lack of vitamin B, and in particular, vitamin B-12 and vitamin B-6.

Human bodies require this vitamin to help in producing red blood cells. Doctors prescribe that our bodies must get at least 2.4 micrograms of this vitamin daily. Since our bodies cannot produce it on their own, we have to consume foods rich in this vitamin.

Since vitamin B-12 is only found in animal products and meat, vegetarians often lack this nutrient. When our bodies do not get enough of this nutrient, the other bodily functions slow down, and not enough red blood cells are produced.

Thus, deficiency can lead to oxygen transport problems. This disorder is known as pernicious anemia, which leads to paranoia, mood swings and depression.

Most of the time, our bodies store a 3-to-5 year worth supply of these nutrients. Thus, symptoms of deficiencies are seen only later on. Deficiency of vitamin B can occur because our bodies are not able to absorb this vitamin. When our bodies lack the enzyme that absorbs the vitamin, we are more prone to depression.

- **Amino acid deficiency:**

Like vitamin B-12, our bodies need nine types of amino acids to function normally. Additionally, these amino acids cannot be produced by our bodies. Thus, we must supply these to our body through proper food choices.

Amino acids help in producing neuro-transmitters that play a part in the proper functioning of our brain. Neurotransmitters are like chemicals; they help in controlling the brain's functions and moods. There are some neurotransmitters that calm the brain and others that excite it. Thus, a proper balance must be maintained to regulate emotional stability. When our bodies lack amino acids, this balance is broken.

Noradrenaline, dopamine and GABA are three important neurotransmitters that are deficient in depressed people. These neuro-transmitters are efficiently produced only by amino acids and vitamins.

Tryptophan and methionine are amino acids that correct disorders like depression and paranoia. Meat, beans, fish and eggs are rich in amino acids. Since we require nine of these acids, you must eat a variety of food to ensure optimal intake.

• **Vitamin-D deficiency:**

Vitamin-D is vital for the proper growth of our bones and immune system. This vitamin helps in optimal brain development. Our brains have receptors, which help in emitting signals to the rest of our body. The signals emitted tell our body exactly how to react to situations. Many parts of our brain have receptors for vitamin-D. These receptors are found in areas of the brain that control your moods.

Doctors suggest that vitamin-D affects chemicals like serotonin and its effect on your brain. When there are low levels of serotonin, we are prone to depression and anxiety. A study conducted in Norway in 2008 showed that people with low levels of vitamin-D showed symptoms of depression.

• **Deficiency of Omega-3 fatty acids:**

This nutrient helps in optimizing the functions of the central nervous system. Scholars have noted that deficiency of omega-3 acids is linked with major depressive disorders.

Doctors state that omega-3 fatty acids help in the conversion of nutrients to mood-enhancing chemicals. A major cause for depression is the imbalance of mood-enhancing chemicals in our body. A study conducted recently concluded that the lack of DHA was closely related to hormonal imbalance. DHA is a type of omega-3 acid that regulates the production of corticotrophin. This is a hormone that moderates the emotional responses of our body. When there is an excess or deficit of this hormone, we are prone to acute mood swings and depression.

When we consume this nutrient, three membranes of our brain are said to function efficiently. Omega-3 fatty acids help in the functioning and development of these membranes.

Flax seeds, cod liver oil and walnuts are rich in this nutrient.

• **Iron deficiency:**
The deficiency of iron causes anemia. It is found that most anemic patients are prone to depression. Iron is required by our body to produce hemoglobin, which is the oxygen compound found in red blood cells. Without this compound, oxygen will not be carried through your bloodstream.

Low iron count leads to improper oxygenation of blood. Doctors have proved that this condition can cause anxiety and panic attacks. This is especially dangerous because prolonged anxiety is known to cause depression. Further, the panic attacks caused by iron deficiency can lead to heart attacks. This is because lack of iron not only leads to psychological problems, but also leads to irregular heartbeats and physical weakness.

Depression can be triggered by thousands of reasons. Sometimes, it could be because of an emotional problem, like the loss of a loved one. This disease is so complex that it makes it hard for a person to predict the cause.

However, doctors have proved that one definite way to combat depression is to eat the right kind of food. This way, your brain wards off negative thoughts and regains emotional stability.

For information on more books, please visit my author page:

http://www.amazon.com/Joe-Mar-tin/e/B00I1FAB2S/ref=ntt_athr_dp_pel_1

www.ingramcontent.com/pod-product-compliance
Lightning Source LLC
Chambersburg PA
CBHW051456170526
45166CB00001B/271